Views of some Eminent people about "Blue book".

The topic is excellent and the contents are v⸻⸻⸻d
Language is very simple and easy-to-unders⸻
For one and all, sequence of thoughts is r⸻
getting digresed.
The book reflects the true and practica⸺ ⸻ ⸻⸻ ⸻e
transformed in practical life very easily.

Gyan Prakash, Director Federation of Indian Chamber of commerce and Industries—FICCI—Rajasthan—Jaipur

* * *

I would recommend to all my friends to look out for excellent piece of work done by Rohit.
To all avid readers "If you wish to find out various hidden aspects of your life, go for it. This will enhance your outlook in a very positive way and make your life much more meaningful.

Dr Ajay Data Founder & CEO Data Infosys limited. Jaipur

* * *

Blue book is a "Life Coach" to pull you out of the blues. It gives a blue print for a successful and content life. The holistic, spiritual and the yogic aspect in today's materialistic world, included in it makes this a unique work book for today's generation.
A man is known by his dreams & vision
"Blue book" tells you how to have both.
You have a life & a "Life Coach: with you.
A "must read must possess" book for anyone aspiring high in life.

Dr Sunil Gupta, MS (ophth) FAGE.
Consultant Opthalmic Surgeon—Jaipur

*   *   *

Blue book is a synopsis of life. It is a guide to the ups and downs in a life cycle in a person's life and also provides the way out or in medical term a treatment or cure for a better life and to face and solve the various problems/ crices we face in a life time . . . . This book will change a person's life and will give him a new focus and energy and will change his way of dealing with other persons and fill his life with love, respect and satisfaction. It is a must read book.

Pankaj Ghiya, Tax Advocate,
President of Rajasthan tax consultant association. Jaipur

*   *   *

In "Blue book", by Shri Rohit kumar vohra has incorporated the lessons learnt by him though experiences he gained during his eventful career spanning over 25 years starting as salesman and going on to become successful entrepreneur. This book is an attempt that will help person to discover themselves and find their best possible way to success.

Dr K.L. Jain,Hony secretary General,
Rajasthan chamber of commerce and industry. Jaipur

*   *   *

Rohit's work is a masterpiece; a powerful blend of deep wisdom and practical lessons of life. His insightful work scratches and surface and moves you at the deepest levels. It's a captivating book which engulfs, entertains and educates. It can enrich and enhance the life of people from all walks of life. Kudos.

Jayshree Periwal
Educationist, Step by Step Groups of School. Jaipur

*   *   *

BLUE BOOK is one of the books that has influenced the simple philosophy behind. I began simplifying my life when I first read this book. It's an easy read and there are some great tips in there.

It's simply life transforming, I was highly enthusiastic about this book when I first read it. It taught me more about compassion than any other book I've read. For that alone, the book is worth its weight in gold.

Shipra bassi, Learned Independent Home maker

*   *   *

The best part of "Blue book" is that it will help many ignorant people to know the importance of soul which is the most important guiding factor of the human life as well as elaborate the importance of God.

This book has shown the way to achive the goal of life "on time" It consists of valuable suggestion to rectify the human error and to achieve the "man—making".

This book carries a lot of potential for the young readers who are on the verge of building their career. I rate this book "AAA" for reader.

A.C Mukerjee, Founder principal,
Swami vivekanand School Ajmer.

*   *   *

Blue book

ROHIT KUMAR VOHRA

PARTRIDGE
A Penguin Company

Partridge books may be ordered through booksellers or by contacting:

Partridge India
Penguin Books India Pvt.Ltd
11, Community Centre, Panchsheel Park, New Delhi 110017
India
www.partridgepublishing.com
Phone: 000.800.10062.62

Contents

SECTION 4

Prologue

Dear Reader, Have you ever thought of aerially visualizing your life through the concept of "Life map"?

Have you ever thought of locating **your position** into such a map of your own life?

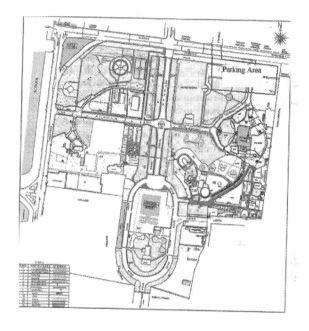

Until you do so—it would not be possible for you to achieve your goal "On time".

First of all, this book suggests you to have an idea of this wonderful and interesting concept, and further it will help you to locate yourself into your own conceptual **"Life's map"**.

Once you identify your present stage out of the "TOPICS" in this book, and by following its few suggestions, you may navigate yourself in a better way—to attain success, or probably 'find a route' to attain success and bliss.

No navigator in the world could ever proceed without knowing or determining its respective present status or location, and this is the simplest method. Surprisingly, most of the people have never focused on this fact when it comes to understand and review their life and its goal.

I have followed and practiced most of the points as mentioned in this book, but "not always".

Whenever I re-read it to contemplate the same, I conceptually grow and get enlightened little more from my previous mental stage, towards realizing these facts.

Let me further assist you by giving an example. Suppose you are in 'crises' during the present phase of your life, then you simply require the topic of "Crises management" of this book, and proceed for the solution. In case you have recently achieved something good, then you may refer to the topic of "Lay down milestones" and proceed with the reading. Suppose you have done something wrong in life, and you do not know what to do next, then simply go to the topic of "Repent without expectation" and proceed further. In case you are lacking self-confidence, then you may refer to the topic of "Gain confidence". Above all, suppose you are at the early stage of life, then just refer to the topic of "Develop a vision" and understand it before following it.

The topics and ideas in this book are expressed in a simple and lucid manner, which are very easy to understand, and may conveniently guide and help the readers to enhance or elevate the quality of their day to day life.

It can be interestingly observed that, this book serves as an abundant source of invaluable ideas which can be considered to have the compilation of timeless and qualitative wisdom of several books. It depends on the propensity of reader that how much inspiration and benefits he try to take out of this book.

All the best!

Rohit Kumar Vohra
Author Jaipur. India
(Age: 42 yrs. Profession: Businessman)

The readership of this book is referred to the targeted age groups which are classified with some Ratings, as under:

'AA' (Very useful): If you are within the age group of 22-30 years.

'A' (Quite useful): If you are within the age group of 30-48 years.

'B' (Very interesting): If you are within the age group of 48 to 55+ years.

'AAA' (Extremely useful): If your age is 55+ then this book is really going to help you for tuning and leading your coming generation on the right track.

This book is an attempt that will help you to discover yourself and find your best suitable way to success, happiness and perhaps to attain Bliss.

*   *   *

Selecting the title of this book as "Blue Book"

Before sending this book for publishing, I gave it to several "Intellectuals" to suggest me the most suitable title for this book. I got various suggestions and few of them are here, as below. But still I could not choose one, since all of them were sounding quite suitable, hence I leave it for you to decide and name it. After all, it is finally your "Blue Book"!

1. Step by step Yogic way to be a successful person
2. Philosophy of life made simple to understand
3. Gateway to Success, Peace and Moksha
4. It is easy to be a successful person
5. Human life and its suitable course
6. To whom so ever it may concern
7. Discover yourself step by step
8. Work, Love, Peace and Moksha
9. The best way to live

After reading and understanding this book, you will think that any of the above titles could be used as the title of this book.

Acknowledgements

First of all, thanks a lot to 'you' (being a reader of this book) for showing interest in this book. Thanks to my Mother Late Sudha, Father Late Mahindra kumar vohra, proffessionl gurus, School,colleage teachers and NCC instructors,They all taught me a lot and also thank to my friends and relatives who read this book before its publication and provided their valuable testimonies and feedback, which encouraged me to write in a more suitable manner for masses.

Thanks to Ms Sadhana Saini, Ms Sapna from Kota, Mr Sumeet from Jaipur for editing the language and my daughter Aasma for finishing the illustration.

Special thanks to my wife Harsha for most of the time listening the topics soon after they were written in odd hours and reading them later critically to give me the feedback.

And above all:

Thank you God for making it possible since you knew it that I wish to do so.

Rohit Kumar Vohra.

Important Note No.1: For Readers

Disclaimer: It is suggested and strongly recommended in expressed/ implied form that, the readers or anyone who follow this book to get all the points/contents (as mentioned in this book) well evaluated/checked by eminent Psychologist elderly people, parents, teachers, mentors, intellectuals or the respective experts, before implementing the theories and practices of this "Blue Book" into one's own life or the others. Author has expressed his own point of view, knowledge and experiences, the effect of which may vary from person to person. The contents of this book are not proven/established facts and hence it does not claim to be 100% correct/suitable for its every reader/follower. Anyone who buy/ read/follow this book, it is assumed that s/he has considered and accepted all the above points, and cannot blame/claim author, editors, publisher and/or any concerning person in any way or to take/charge for the losses/ damages (if any) of any kind, anytime, anywhere or in any manner expressed/implied whatsoever.

Important Note No.2: For Readers

Each one of us is at some specific point (in our life), as mentioned in either of the topics/chapters which is referred as phase or stage of our life. Identify yourself "where you are" in the journey of your life, understand the "stage" and move ahead accordingly. If your life is more messed up then start your "new life-journey" from the topic No. 1 and go on . . . . It is never late to "restart", once you restart you have a greater chance to get the success and to get blessed and move towards attaining the "Bliss".

Human life has four components at large:

- Mind
- Body
- Heart
- Soul

Mind: It is nurtured and developed by a person on the basis of the fundaments which he has inherited through his DNA or learnt through his parents in addition to his elementary education and social environment. A person is the sole owners of his mind and responsible for all of its acts.

Body: Body is gifted to us by our parents.

Heart: Philosophically, here this component is not referred to an organ which a person has inside his chest. It means a place of one's emotions and feeling 'within the mind'. It is solely developed by one's sub-consciousness and nurtured with love and happiness. It is referred to person's choices, likings and such an emotional part (aspect) of brain which helps a person to take several such decisions that a mind cannot process, because the working of mind concerns deals with facts and figures, intellect and the conscious efforts.

Soul: It is the best part of all the four components, and it is gifted to us by Almighty God through our parents, in the form of a life force spread over to each and every cell and the genetic material of our body. The passive form of a soul gets a chance to be carried along or placed into the reproductive cells of parents which further transforms into the dynamic life force of a conceived child (fetus).

Knowledge of mind and body is clearly understood by most of us, but the spiritual knowledge about existence, origin and importance of soul is not so clearly known to many people. It can be conceptually compared with an example of a SIM card in a cell phone, some people know about the mobile handset with loaded software in it, but they do not know much about SIM card and how does it work? In this example, SIM card to the mobile handset can be correlated with the importance of soul to the human and other living beings. Knowledge about existence of soul also manifests the importance of Almighty God.

In this book, I am trying to elaborate the importance of God, who gifted us the soul as a life force of our existence.

We owe a lot to our Parents and the Almighty God, who have given us wonderful body and super wonderful soul.

SECTION 1

Understanding "Blue Book"

My Dear Reader, After reading this book, you might get answers to various questions, which probably many people wanted to ask. These answers are written in a very simple language, to facilitate the understanding of a person having an average IQ. You may create any question related to your present life and might get the relevant answer in some form in this book.

This book conveys the philosophical-cum-practical aspect of human life. It depends upon the reader's perceptions (while reading this book) that how he reaps the benefits out of this book. You may get the answers as per your perception. This book may truly become a very useful book for the readers if they keep their attitude positive towards the author. Inferences and interpretations will vary from person to person.

This book is about the philosophy of human life, and this is actually a self-help book. This is my first attempt to write and convey my message, views on human life through a book. This book offers some basic guidelines to be followed and placed in person's life.

Today At the time of start(in 2006) I am a successful businessman of 42 years, with an experience of 21 years of hardships in life. During these 21 years, I had been a salesman, a manager, an entrepreneur, on the job trainer, an advertiser, apart from being a cook, pilot, musician, stage actor, sportsperson, swimmer, horse rider and a successful NCC cadet of National level. I have worked with several types of people and have been training them for several tasks, be it selling, human resources development, debt recovery methods, launching of new concepts, dealing with labour, Government officers to ministers and lawyers, from creative writing in advertisement agency to planning, developing infrastructure, doing door-to-door sales to International business, media planner to a successful negotiator.

The two factors which I followed common in every task were: optimism and hard work. Optimistic approach was very much required to accomplish any tasks while putting in hard work. I shared this very message with "One and all". Today, most of them (including me) are living happy and successful life.

Apart from doing hard work and following an optimistic approach, it is the destiny which plays the role of a "better half" in our lives. There is no substitute of destiny. Out of 100 marks in the "exam" of our lives, we are capable of achieving only 49 marks at the most and rest 51 marks are in the hands of our destiny.

Each one of us must accept the fact that despite of pouring in our best inputs into any activity, we have control only over 49% of the task, and the rest 51% is ruled and controlled by our destiny. That's why at the end of our sincere effort and hard work, we look upon destiny for the results.

You might have come across some of those people in your life who may not be as hard working as you, but still they are more successful! Yes, it happens because their destiny favors them more than 51% for sure.

"Why does it happen like this . . . ," could be a question of yours. And you may find the answer in the coming pages. I would have given the answer here itself, but I am sure you would have not taken it "as it is". Before I answer such a question of yours, I would have to guide and elevate you mentally up to such a level where it would be rather easy for you to understand and accept it.

Destiny plays a crucial role in defining the course of our lives. None of us are sure about what percentage of destiny we actually have. It may differ from situation to situation. We should not stop putting our inputs and efforts into our course of action, knowing that its results are not in our control. I would rather insist that we must give our best because we are capable of doing it and rest everything may be left on God.

We can get inspiration from the world famous proverb that, "God helps those who help themselves."

How this book can help a Reader?

In today's scenario, people who are unsuccessful and unhappy are so because they are confused or they do not follow the correct course of action. Majority of confused people say that, "We are right in our perspective." Such people actually do not evaluate the facts and contemporary changes meticulously.

Each one of us must know about our respective positions in the map of our life that, "Where I am, and what are my 'related' strengths?"

"Where I am" means the position/location/junction in the journey of life, and you should also know about your navigation power and skills, and "then only" proceed further in right direction to take RIGHT STEP AT THE RIGHT TIME, else you will land up on a dead end, and will have to re-start from the zero level again.

This book is intended to help every reader, no matter which walk of life s/he represents—whether the reader be a student or a businessman, a house wife or a lady, a minister; the rules remain the same for all. The book can easily help and guide them to proceed further step by step and be a successful person in his/her respective field. It is possible only then when all the relevant steps (as mentioned in this book) are truly and completely implemented.

Author strongly recommends the readers to please re-notify the **"Important Note No.1: For Readers"** as mentioned earlier in this book.

☺ Thanks ☺

"Blue Book"

Quite frankly, "To whom so ever it may concern" might have been the most suitable title for this wonderful book. For a simple reason, this book makes sense to its each and everyone who reads it.

It took about 15 years for me to authoritatively start writing this book. These 15 years were my learning and observation period before I could say about, whatever, I have finally written. I am neither a professional writer, nor a philosopher, but I think that each one of us, who has the flair to express oneself, may become a writer and a philosopher in his own special manner. The thought of sharing certain experiences was a single reason to write this book. Today I am a businessman who started his career as a simple door-to-door salesperson on a monthly salary of Rs 500 or (12 USD) in the year 1985. With the grace of God, blessings of my parents, and support of my wife and brother, I am taking care of a small size of company now. This business is of an Ayurvedic dental tooth powder and paste, namely—"YDM-YUNADENT", which I am operating in few states of India, along with a product & brand development consultant to few companies, along with a distribution of Organic products, Such a phase (junction) is not even the one-tenth of my dream goal, but it seems enough for me to survive in this lifetime.

Writing this book was also one of the goals of my life. During past 15 year, I used to write quotations as a gist of my thought process, and I had the aspirations to elaborate my all such writings one day with real life situations and illustrations.

The caption "Blue Book" is not my biography in any way, but it has definitely to do something with you! Yes you, as a reader of this book. Naming this book as "Blue Book" had a simple reason of using the word—blue, which means nude. In other words, the blue signifies—without any cover. "Blue print" means the innermost structural layout. The "Blue Book" in the corporate world means the book of norms and guidelines. This book is written directly to the point and focussed on the relevant topics. No preface to any point is written but it has just been stated in a straight forward manner as per my personal views about the topic. In case you consider the contents and description of this book as correct, it would mean that you have touched or reached to the "Blue" point of your life.

Now I take you to the main subject. The subject is about life, "The philosophy of human life". This book can be read as many times until it is properly understood and positively interpreted for getting implemented into your life because without harmonizing with its thought process and its suggested ways, it would not only be difficult to attain success and happiness but it will take more time too.

Principally if you are in agreement with this book, I am sure that whenever you would read this book, you would get "yet another" meaning each time, and it will help you to grow further towards your goal.

As a basic norm, kindly fill in the blanks of the questionnaire mentioned ahead, and if possible either send it to the author or visit www. rohitbluebook.com to fill in the answers in its questionnaire. While reading this book, refer your answers repeatedly and further correlate with author's point of view. However, author will try to respond to your questions through www.rohitbluebook.com

I am quite sure that if you wish to reach a particular destination in a 'new city' or a city where you have never been before, or a city which is not 'well known' to you, and if you are given a map of the city as a help, you would reach your destination conveniently in least possible time.

Unfortunately, if you do not get such a map then you would not only take a lot of time to reach your destination but you might even get lost, or you would continue asking people about the address where you wish to reach. Such a lengthy process might be quite time consuming, grueling and full of hassles.

Hope, you agree . . . !

If I am right then let me further share my (author's) modus operandi with you. First of all, I would ask you to search your status/location in the journey of your life, and then from there onwards, I suggest you a suitable way to reach your destination. For this I would need your help.

This search of mine will not only let me understand your location in life, but in this course you would also discover yourself and this is the most important factor, as the first step.

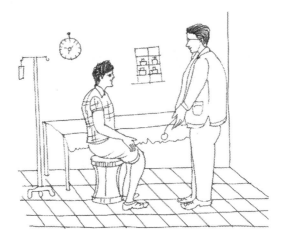

It can further be simplified by giving an example of a doctor and a patient. Suppose a patient having pain in stomach visits a doctor for consultation, then first of all doctor asks a patient about the problem and then clinically examines the patient while asking few relevant questions. A patient may be asked to lie down on the observation table in supine position so as to physically examine (palpate) patient's stomach, and then doctor may ask few important questions, such as:

- What & where did you eat?
- Did you over eat?
- Did you take your last meal quite late, or against the schedule?
- Did you do so and so . . . ?

Such a question and answer session actually confirms the patient that doctor has understood his problem. As far as doctor is concerned, it helps him to find out the cause of illness and to give an optimal treatment to the patient. With the answers to such questions, both the doctor and the patient get satisfied for having understood each other.

Patient then asks, "Ok Doctor, please prescribe me the medicines, and what should I abstain so as to recover my health and fitness." Doctor then prescribes medical treatment and a regimen for the patient.

The above example or process may be referred or transposed to other similar situations, such as, when you visit to consult an astrologer or a palmist.

In the same way, I would like to understand about you by exploring few aspects of your mind or thought process. **It will also help you to discover about the hidden and interesting aspects of your own good self**. I would be able to find out and suggest you a route to happiness and success through this as per your specific requirements.

To discover about the unexplored facets of your own unique and special personality, you need to answer the questionnaire as mentioned in next few pages.

Thanks, once again.

Discovery of your personality

(Consider you are in egg, from egg to nest, nest to tree, tree to sky)

Part-1

Questionnaire No.1: Spiritual Quotient (S.Q.) Level

Important Notes:

- Please do not share this page with anybody else, after answering the questionnaire
- Do not try to answer in order to impress the examiner (including yourself)

Time limit: (No time limit)

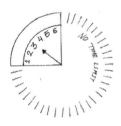

Date: _____   Name: _____

Answer the first 10 Questions by rating questions **on the scale of 1 to 100** as follows:

1. How much do you believe that there are four components of your life: "Mind, Body, Heart and Soul"?
    Answer _____

2. How much do you believe that you are remotely controlled by a supernatural power?
    Answer _____

3. How much do you believe that you have got a predestined number of seconds, called the Age in other words, for your life?
    Answer _____

4. How much do you believe that God exists everywhere?
    Answer _____

5. How much do you believe that the consequences are carried on even to your next birth or life?
   Answer _____

6. How much do you believe that your deeds are directly related to your family and supporters?
   Answer _____

7. How much do you believe that one can understand God or supernatural power within the span of one human life itself?
   Answer _____

8. How much do you believe in a feeling of general mass that places of worship such as temples and pilgrimages have their own incomparable worth?
   Answer _____

9. How much do you believe that there is a solution to every problem?
   Answer _____

10. How much do you agree that "truth & truthfulness" is the biggest strength and power above all?
    Answer _____

Part-2

Questionnaire No.1 continues . . .

Answer the next Question Nos. 11 to 21 in least possible words. The lengthy answers will have "negative marking". Try to answer in very short and get the best out of you.

11. What is your biggest wish?
    Answer _____
    _____

12. What is the aim of your life?
    Answer _____
    _____

13. Why do you want to live?
    Answer _____
    _____

14. What satisfies you?
    Answer _____
    _____

15. Why and when do you generally face problems in your life?
    Answer _____
    _____

16. Quote your unsolvable problem in few words only?
    Answer _____
    _____

17. If you perceive and believe in God, then what would be your first reaction if God appears in front of you, as per its image in your mind?
    Answer _____
    _____

18. What does happiness means to you?
    Answer _____
    _____

19. What brings you happiness?
    Answer _____
    _____

20. What would you like to leave behind after you death?
    Answer _____
    _____

21. What would you like to do, if an option is given to rewind and rework your life?
    Answer _____
    _____

Now, the most important Question:

22. Kindly ask any question of your choice, just any question from the universe. Question (Please ask):
    _____
    _____

    Answer: <u>You might get the answer from this book, or you would get the reference as a clue to find your answer.</u>

Date: _____   Your Signature _____

Note 1 → In Part-1, if your total count is:

- Less than 500, then you need consultancy
- Between 500 to 700, then you need to do introspection by now
- Between 700 to 900, then you just need bit of a support system to be a successful person
- Between 900-1000, then you well understand things and you are not less than a successful person

Note 2 → In Part-2, your answers will help you to do self-analysis.

Note 3 → In Part-3 (as follows), your answers will help you to draw your life line to success.

Part-3

Questionnaire No.2: Discovery continues . . .

Answer these Questions preferably one day after doing Exercise No.1.

Question No.1. Who are you? (Please think thrice before writing this simple answer)

Answer _____
_____
_____
_____

Question No.2. What is your address? (Please think thrice before writing this simple answer, most of people give their residential or office address here if unfortunately today you are a victim of an earth quake and you loose your house and office both will you be address less??, where as in this question objective is to know your address in this 'universe' and 'your mental and social' stage of life—where you are standing as of now)

Answer _____
_____
_____
_____

Question No.3. What is your biggest strength and why?

Answer _____
_____
_____
_____

Human life is a Great Journey

Human life is a great journey, and the various phases (junctions) in this journey forms a huge journey cycle. This cycle can be called "Brahma Chakra" (the spiritual circle). No one really knows that up to which junction he will reach, but one must have a desire and courage to go as far as possible in this journey.

We have to keep going and moving because our actual 'active life span' is an active part of it, and this active part is the journey of "Chakra".

The sequence of junctions could be as per following pattern, which I refer as the probable "Brahma Chakra/Yatra" (Spiritual Circle/Journey) in correspondence with the courage and help of our inner strengths. These junctions keep changing their sequence, and they are not under control of your personal choice. Life itself lifts and shifts a person as s/he acquires knowledge and fulfils the responsibilities.

If a person jumps from one junction to another by wrong means and ways, then such a new junction itself re-dresses (re-destines) a person by sending to a lower or different junction, as suitable.

Each junction demands 'its value' from each one of us. One who fulfils can stay and grow on the respective junction, and over a period of time such a junction itself shifts you to the better one. But if one cannot or does not perform as per need of the junction, then a person gets shifted to a suitable one and this new junction is generally either lower or harder one because it happens to be a sort of punishment for those who could not perform as desired by the junction.

Similarly in another case, if you are ruled by "Greed" and decide to jump to a new junction, then you would also get a similar treatment later on because the rule is broken by yourself as you decided to unfairly jump on a new junction of your choice. You are very well aware of the present status of your life. Now what is to be done next, and what exactly had happened before you came to the present situation of life. On the basis of answers to these questions, you can decide your current line of action to attain happiness and success.

Please take care of yourself, give an extra serving of thought to your invaluable life. I wish Good Luck for your life, and for the coming junctions in it.

Do not let your life to get driven in the Vicious circle. Try and remain in Natural circle.

Being natural is a way of life!

Probable "Brahma Chakra" (Spiritual Life Cycle)

The "Brahma Chakra" probably has 12 junctions (stages) in series. These junctions are in increasing order of their importance, and so each subsequent junction is higher than its previous one. We can get naturally elevated to next higher junction, after attaining the essence and fulfilling the requirements of each specific junction. These junctions (stages) are as follows:

1. ***Jeev*** (Human/One's present status): First of all, we are a human being, which means *Jeev* in Hindi language.
2. ***Anuyayi*** (The follower): It is a disciple of ethical human life.
3. ***Sevak*** (The servant): At this stage, one can become the servant of a specific community. It is explained in this book later on.
4. ***Wachak*** (The preacher): At this stage we can become narrator of an ideology such as described in this book. (**Author is on this stage.**)
5. **Guru** (A Hindu spiritual teacher or the super preacher, is called Guru): After attaining the status of a preacher, one can become a Guru, such as, Guru of sun signs (planets' behavior), Guru of Astrology, Guru of Yoga and Guru of all four Vedas, or Guru of your own field.
   After reaching at the level of Guru within this life span, one has a very big chance to attain Moksha (the salvation, or an ultimate state of peace—The Bliss). You can see so many people in your country at this level.
6. ***Sant/Pantik/Sadhu*** (Saint, or community creator): Once we attain the position as Guru in the society, one can become a community creator like, Jesus Christ, Prophet Mohammad, Gautam Buddha. One has higher chances to attain Moksha at this junction. *Sadhu* means one who renounces his life. One can become a *Sadhu* and renounce the world to move on the path of attaining Moksha, by leaving behind a community who believe in

his teachings and practice the teachings forever. You can see some of them in current scenario in the world, like, Mahatma Gandhi, Swami Vivekananda, etc.

7. ***Gyanendra*/Rishi** (Human with vast spectrum of knowledge): A person can become *Gyanendra*/Rishi at this stage. Such a status is attained by a very few as written in Vedas and Upanishads, or they were Parshuram, Ravana, Barbareek, Vishwakarma, etc. as per Hindu spiritual mythologies.

We surely get Moksha at this stage.

8. ***Grah*** (The planet): At this stage, one can get an infinite position in the universe, such as, *Sapt Rishis, Dhruva, Rahu, Ketu, Shani,* Venus, Mars and others, as per Hindu spiritual mythology.

9. ***Dev*** (Deity): We can still go beyond this junction within this human life with the same soul and get a position of *Devta* (God man) or *Devi* (Goddess), such as, incarnations of Shri Ganesh, Shri Hanuman, Maa Saraswati, Maa Vaishnovi are the few names from Hindu spiritual mythology.

10. ***Brahmananda*** (Universal awareness, or the power of Moksha): One who has the super most happiness and peace is being described here as *Brahmananda*. We can become *Brahmananda*. At this junction you become one of the powers without which this universe is incomplete and take the shape of shapeless, such as, fire, air, water, earth or sky which are called *Pancha bhoot*. One can become a part of Brahma at this junction (stage).

11. **Brahma** (The generator or creator of universe): After the above 10 junctions (stages), we get merged into Brahma as the generator or creator of universe. Lord Brahma is the father or generator of the universe.

    The above journey through 11 junctions (stages) of the Soul life is possible which starts from as a *Jeev* (a human being).

    God—Who is it then? If all above 11 junctions (stages) have covered everything in the universe, then what is such a junction? What all a God can do? How it is above 11th junction (stage) of life—Brahma? How does this power operate? What kind of shape it has? Where does it exist? There can be several trillion questions about God!

12. **God (GOD**—The word can be deduced to be an acronym for **G**enerator, **O**perator & **D**estroyer): Beyond the stage of Brahma, one can further get upgraded and merged into God. At this

junction, after getting merged into God, we become the core tiny part and parcel of the supernatural power called the Almighty God.

I underwent deep contemplation several times during the course of my life, after observing thousands of things with my **Sixth sense***. I tried to make a sequence of thoughts which has no external parameters. Then experiencing the same, I reached to the following conclusion as my first version of understanding of this power which I am keen to share with you by giving several day-to-day examples.

*(Sixth sense: God has gifted this sense to each one of us, and we need to explore it.)

There are many names given to God by different communities and religions. Surprisingly most of them have realized that God is one (not more than one), and this supreme power has several potentials and versatilities.

Let's understand something about God.

In Hindu spirituality, this almighty power or God is called *Bhagwan (Parampita Parmeshwar)*. God can be explained with respect to its following aspects:

Param Racheita **(Almighty Generator):** One who can generate or create anything in any shape, size or form for any utility (as written on previous 11th junction (stage), Brahma is one part).

Param Palak **(Almighty Operator):** One who can remotely operate his creation by the supernatural means.

Param Vinashak **(Almighty Destroyer):** One who can destroy anything or everything as per his own wish in a spur of the moment and can create a cause for any destruction at any junction.

The first three stages or aspects (as above) are the prime introductions about **GOD**. The word therefore can be deduced to be an acronym for the **G**enerator, **O**perator & **D**estroyer.

There are 9 major factors of *Bhagwan* as follows:

Param Karak (**Almighty Logical**): One who has reasons and logics for all of his acts, and can explain the same to the complete satisfaction of all the creatures.

Param Karta (**Almighty work performer, or the Omnipotent**): One who can perform any work and who can describe the link between everything in the universe with each other.

Param Gyanak (**Almighty Knowledgeable, or the Omniscient**): One who has the tiniest, finest and the largest controlling knowledge of each and every molecule existing in this universe.

Param Sukshma (**Almighty Tiniest**): One who can be seen or felt at its tiniest (essence) form. It is the essence of anything or everything in this universe.

Param Vyapak (**Almighty Spread, or the Omnipresent**): One who is omnipresent, which means, it is present anywhere and everywhere at the same time, in several forms of life, things and power.

Param Atma (**Almighty Soul**): One who has the sole control on all the souls existing in human beings, including living creatures, fauna, avifauna, flora, etc because each and every existing soul is the tiny released part of the Almighty Soul. It also includes the souls of the spirits (non-bodily souls) which might be at transition/non-living phase between death and life (rebirth), or higher spiritual junctions, or the stage of attaining salvation!

All of these souls, powers and shapes are the part and partial of *Param Atma*. Therefore, apart being a core part of its own existence, *Param Atma* also exists as the essence, nuclear or an infinitesimal part of every living being in the form of a soul. The soul stays in *Jeev* and again this great journey of Brahma Chakra continues . . . !

Getting back to *Jeev*

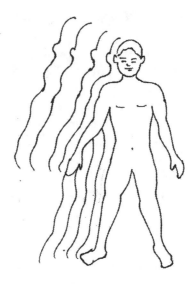

We remain a passenger of this great life cycle until we get a Moksha. Our life remains in this great journey, as if we are sitting in a non-stop roller-coaster or non-stop rotating swing. How long can we sit in this swing or roller-coaster? Have you ever realized this? Would you like to accept this fact?

Just think about it!

In this great journey, most of us do not realize the actual status of our own, and we die in the vicious circle of common human life. We should go beyond the present junction to discover ourselves and our knowledge and further proceed towards the 11th stage of "Brahma Chakra". For such a holy and great mission, God surely blesses its followers.

One (especially, citizens of Western countries) might ask a simple question that, "How can I reach all the junctions (as above) especially, *Dev, Grah* and further from there onwards . . . ? I have never seen, read or heard in my life about anybody reaching those junctions. It is either myth or mythological stories!"

I can assist you by clarifying your doubt with a simple example. Just go to any of the most remote village of any state (in the map) where even the very basic facilities of electricity and roads are not available. (Such villages can be seen in any of the various under-developed countries.)

After reaching there, search a young kid of 10 years, and ask him about mobile phone, internet, microwave oven, robots, fully-automatic washing machine, and computer with mobile connectivity. He will sure look at you quite strangely. He will think that, either you are an insane person or some exorcist. But, when you show him such items along with explaining him systematically all about the same with lots of relatively common logics, examples, proofs and efforts, that these types of things and apparatus do exists and work as per our command, then he will not only get convinced and mesmerized, but he would also get lost with no words to say. He might be left with his wide-open eyes and mouth in front of you, and you would still wait for his confirmation or acceptation about your description.

I assume that most of the people are actually equivalent to such a 10 year old kid from a remote village, who cannot understand the junctions beyond their thinking in the field of spirituality. I can demonstrate God in the similar way (as you would have done in front of that kid about your apparatus), but you would not accept it like the same kid of 10 years, hence you need to experience it to believe it by living your entire life consciously and relate your life to God's power on day-to-day basis. The same theory applies to all 12 junctions (stages) of "Brahma Chakra", which are beyond the understanding of any reader who has doubts. Once you reach at 2nd junction you can easily see the path of 3rd, and once you reach at 3rd you can easily see the path of 4th, and so on.

Here onwards, I will help you to explore your present junction and discuss the topic of the junction called *Jeev*. I will try to create a map where you would be able to identify your own location, and then I will guide you about the way beyond which you would be able to develop your own capacity for getting a route to next junction, and then gradually to the subsequent higher junctions.

SECTION 2

Your "Blue Book" and You

I do not know that how many versions I would be able to write after this "Blue Book—2011". I am sure I will keep exploring and writing about the junctions.

You should continue to read this book further only if all the matter (as written in SECTION—1) sounds good to you. Else, please leave it as a read newspaper.

My humble request, kindly follow few basic guidelines while reading this book.

First of all, please write your name in the blank space as follows:

My _____'s Blue Book

PLEASE observe and follow the points as under:

- ✓ Try to read this book in a quiet, calm and comfortable environment (preferably early morning), or while travelling, or at a place where you have the least chances of getting disturbed.
- ✓ While reading, try to make your thought process absolutely normal and neutral. It is quite possible that you might not be convinced with my thoughts and ideas, but I request you to understand the gist of the script without prejudice.
- ✓ Kindly take a pencil and underline the sentences which you think that, "Yes, I fully agree to it, or it is really a new discovery for me, or it is really a wonderful learning just written for me."
- ✓ Until you completely understand the topic, please do not proceed further. There is no hurry to finish this book. Try to think along, but if you think that you want to finish it once, and you would give a deeper thought while re-reading it the next time, then you can follow your choice.

- ✓ Please write your name in this blank space: _____, if you missed it before.
- ✓ To really understand this book as a thought process, please read it at least two-times.
- ✓ Second last request: Try to read this book as slow as possible, as if you are narrating this book in a class room, may be 6th standard of a school.
- ✓ Last request: The sequence shown in this book is actually the best assumed sequence of life, if you are in your early stage of life you can start from "Self-respect".

In case you are way beyond and somewhere on 6th or 10th or may be on 12th stage as per the sequence of this book, then it is recommended to follow the onwards stages as suggested in the book, for example, if you are on 12th stage of life which is "Crises management", then it is recommended by author to understand crises management and further follow the subsequent stage "Worship your God". This way, you will remain on the right or best possible track to success, and finally to Bliss.

Your location!

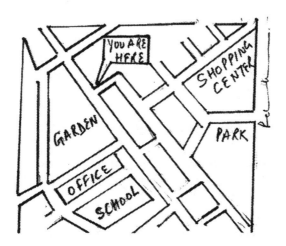

First of all, whenever you look at to any Road Map to reach somewhere, you check your own location in the map and then you plan to reach to your destination. Similarly, to plan your life further, you should find your location (status or condition) at this point of time in the Map of your Life, and then you decide about the goal. In fact you should definitely know about your goal.

Until you really know about the exact location (where you are) in the present situation of life, you should not proceed further.

Once again I highlight the gist of initial few paragraphs on page No.1 of this book, that each one of us are somewhere (location) on either of the topics (stages) as mentioned in SECTION-3 of this book. Identify your location/stage (correlating to the topics of SECTION-3) in the journey of your life, understand the same and move ahead accordingly. If your life is more messed up then start your "new life-journey" from the topic No. 1 and go on. It is never late to "restart". Once you restart, you have a greater chance to get success and move towards attaining the Bliss.

Most of us are actually the patients (sufferers) of any specific disease (problem)—be it a mental, physical or social. Generally, our attitude remains the same for the both—whether it is a disease or a problem. First of all, we have to recognize the disease, then take the consultation, medication, and follow the abstinence guidelines respectively. And then only we can get cured.

Some people do not even accept the fact that they have any disease (problem). If some people recognize their disease, then due to negligence they do not sincerely try to get rid of it, or they do not have the courage to discipline themselves for taking medication, guidelines and follow a treatment regimen. It is important that we should not only recognize a disease (problem) but also follow its complete course of medicine and regimen sincerely, so as to get cured (solve the problem) and become fit (to proceed further) for achieving our dream goals.

It is a spiritualistic truth that we are not born to earn or acquire more and more material wealth in this world. We should surly acquire several other wealth too.

You would agree with me that in modern life scenario, material wealth is the only parameter which is considered by most people as best parameter to evaluate one's success. So it has become the foremost priority. Most of us spend our complete life in matching this materialistic priority only.

Material wealth is surely required up to a good extent as a necessity and to live a decent quality of life in this materialistic world, but acquiring 'only' the materialistic wealth is actually a very small and short-sighted goal taking the life as a whole.

Several invaluable wealth which one must acquire, are as under:

- ✓ Wealth of love, long-term happiness and stable peace
- ✓ Wealth of knowledge and truthfulness
- ✓ Wealth of having a power to serve humanity and its derived satisfaction after having done it
- ✓ Wealth of power to serve in canvassing the virtue of God and his aura for the welfare of humanity
- ✓ Wealth in form of our journey towards attaining Moksha

No material—whether it a highly furnished house, car, property or a huge bank balance can give us the permanent prosperity, happiness, peace or love in life. Then why should we blindly keep running after the materialistic wealth and collecting their better and better versions unnecessarily in excess. No man-made material in this world has ever existed which can give the long-term happiness, stable peace, ever growing knowledge, way to walk with truthfulness, power to serve mankind or God.

As we are on the first stage of our life journey cycle, it is difficult to really get what we wish so easily. We should understand about our present status of life, and try to get success as we deserve and then re-understand the entire theory of life.

I strongly believe that after reading, understanding and following this book step-by-step, you will be able to fulfill utmost of your desires. Therefore, let's find out the present position of our great human life journey as *Jeev* (The living being).

Stage / Junction No.1
Normal living being, or *Sadharan Jeev*

Any creature having a potential of life, a body in which the soul stays and live for a specific period called *Jeev* (normal living being), and it is you, me and everybody around us, be it a human or an animal, insect, bird, etc. As human beings, we have this opportunity to understand ourselves and pass on the knowledge earned to the coming generation for their upliftment. We have got a supernatural latent power as talent, and we must discover all the covers which have covered us. These covers are the clouds of darkness and foolishness. We are humans, the ever best-known creatures of universe, the ever-best machine known that exists anywhere in the universe, then why to waste precious short-lived life for anything else other than knowing yourself, uplifting yourself, devoting yourself to create a happy, healthy, satisfying and peaceful life. All of us will die one day, and none of us really knows till when we are alive. We have a human body given by our parents and we have a soul within us gifted by Almighty God. Practically, only mind is ours that is cultured by us as a driver to this life. Should we allow this driver to waste our life in collecting the materialistic things created by another human? Or, let's create a wealth which is never going to be finished and let this wealth grow more by consuming it.

Surprisingly, the knowledge alone is such a wealth which grows through consumption. Keep acquiring it and keep it passing on. None other but the *Gyan* (knowledge) wealth is going to grow. All other forms of wealth, be it money, health, name or fame are going to vanish one day, but not the *Gyan*.

Knowledge is considered to be the perpetual wealth.

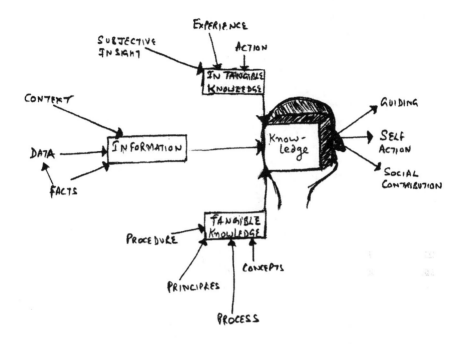

I further share my knowledge with you (which I have acquired over the period of last 30 years) to assist you to achieve your desired goals.

Being a *Jeev* actually means that we have two major potentials in our life. Firstly, we can become successful for ourselves and for our coming generation in our family. Secondly, we can become much more than a *Sadharan Jeev* and attain Bliss.

Since we are normal human beings and we have got lots of desires for ourselves, including, the greed, anger and emotions which suppresses, drifts or confuses us. That is why we find it a bit difficult to deal and grow in both of the above two major potentials.

31

SECTION 3

Something about SECTION 3

In various Topics in this section, I further try and assist you in achieving your dreams and become a successful person, then later in this book I will suggest and guide you a path that can elevate you from normal human being to a state of Blissful human being.

To whom so ever it may concern! To live a normal human life we must follow such a course of life which makes our life go smooth. We all are working for good health, better comforts and better goodwill.

There may be several ways to look at anything, and any of such way is known as the 'point of view'. Everybody has a view point, but a view point which is most suitable in given circumstances makes sense.

'Sequence' of the points (topics) that are commonly seen as the background story of a successful person are mentioned further, along with their step-by-step description.

You as a reader of this book have to identify your stage in the journey of your life, to proceed further.

TOPICS

1. Know your present status—Think deep
2. Have self-respect—If you lack
3. Should have a dream—If you lack
4. Develop a vision—If you lack
5. Gain confidence—If you are under-confident
6. Just work hard—If you are a lazy person
7. Confrontation is a part of life—Don't feel shy to do so
8. Happiness is the key word—If you are sad or does not frequently feel happy
9. Faith, nothing has worth without it—If you have lost it
10. Developing devotion—If you lack

11. Facing the failure—If you have failed
12. Crises management—If you are in a crisis
13. Worship your God—If you are not repeller
14. Realize without prejudice—If you have done a mistake
15. Repent without expectation—Must do
16. Rectify by heart—That is the way
17. Love has no substitute—Maintain your love
18. Be happy again—Happiness is the best fuel
19. Desire instead of being greedy—Evaluate the difference
20. Never lose the self-esteem—Stick to your fundamental ethics
21. Struggling is a part of the game—Keep pouring in
22. Patience—It is a virtue
23. Differentiate between Smart and Hard work—Differentiate
24. Focus on the task—If you tend to lose focus or have multifocal attitude
25. Regaining confidence—If you have lost it
26. Habit of winning—Keep improving your skills
27. Lay down milestones—If you are stagnated
28. Build your Fort—If you want to secure yourself
29. Shine as a star and spread like air—You need to set example and proceed
30. Renounce it (The semi-final word)—You need to leave for next generation
31. Get dissolved (It is the final word)—You need to get Bliss

Let's understand the topics one by one . . .

1. Know your present status—Think deep

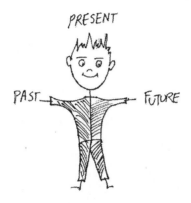

As mentioned earlier, when we wish to go somewhere then it is very important for us to understand about our location in the Map. Once we know about it, then only we can make a route to reach our dream destination. Isn't it a simple fact? Now visualize your life and society as a huge Map, if you need to get something or the status of your desire. To proceed further, you should understand your present status with the help of relevant questions, such as:

➢ What are your working strengths?
➢ What are your limitations?
➢ What do you want to achieve?
➢ What are your talents, or strengths, or the qualities that you have got as a God gift?
➢ Why do you really want "that" specific thing?
➢ What made you choose "that" specific goal for yourself?
➢ How do you analyze your past 5-10 years?
➢ Finally, where you are (or, on which stage you are) out of the **topics** listed in this "Blue Book"?

These are few basic questions which can help you to proceed further. You can form few more questions of your own to understand your present status. If you are unable to answer the above questions, or if you think that you have never given such type of answers then at least try to answer one question to yourself—"What are my strengths?"

I suggest you must take a diary and write all answers to the questions as asked in previous paragraph, including your own formed questions.

2. Have self-respect—If you lack

Each one of us lives and leads our life on the basis of knowledge earned and used for any aspect of life. As a matter of fact, all of us are the part and parcel of unique sequence of life. It is a huge circle and there are various circles inter-linked with each other, and we keep working towards the predictable direction in a disorientated manner! At the end of radius we enter in the next new circle. This act keeps on going and we keep moving from one circle to another. One can call it a phase, a semester, a mini junction or the circumstances of our lives.

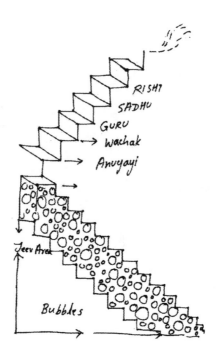

To understand it further, let's assume that you are in a room which is filled with lots of bubbles, amongst which, some of them are small-sized, some are medium-sized, and rest are big bubbles. Now assume yourself to be a tiny creature living inside one of these bubbles and gradually crawling along its wall. After some time, you would move into other bubble, and then to yet another one and this sequence would continue to go on further. You could change bubble after bubble and your life ends in one of these bubbles. At the end of life, one could die in any one of such three types of bubbles, which could be:

(1) Smaller size of bubble,

Small-Bubble

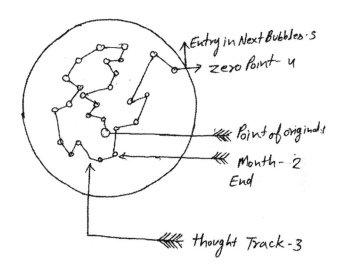

Entry in Next Bubbles - 5

zero Point - 4

Point of original 1

Month - 2
End

thought Track - 3

MAX Bubble life, 2 years
Averg1 ,, ,, 1 Years
MIN ,, ,, 3 Month - 6 month

(2) Bigger size of bubble

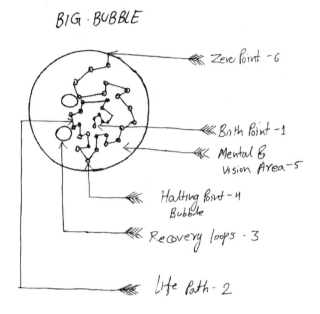

BIG · BUBBLE

≪ Zero Point -6

≪ Birth Point -1

≪ Mental &
Vision Area -5

≪ Halting Point - 4
Bubble

≪ Recovery loops - 3

≪ Life Path - 2

(3) Same size of bubble from where you began.

If we restrain our lives only up to the materialistic facets of these bubbles, then it may seem to be quite worthless in spiritual and moral pursuits.

It is a truth that the journey of ethical and spiritual enlightenment of our lives can elevate us to a peaceful, blissful state, and further. Let's come out of the typically motivated materialistic life and live a better life. Draw your correct line of action, and it is simple. In case you have already understood it, then I congratulate you for having identified your correct and meaningful objective in life.

The universal truths and life are basically very simple. We make our life complicated just due to the lack of our own clarity. What all is required, is to understand the simplicity of universal law.

Just look around yourself. Everything created by God is simple and you can understand it by just applying common sense (which is not that common). You would realize that universal laws are very simple and so is the life. This simplicity will help you to make your life simple and successful, for example, this earth was at one point of time full of wildlife, ever since then we have developed million times better now. Such a growth took place slowly and gradually in several millenniums and that too in various small phases. In a similar way, if we wish to get the best out of us, or to contribute our best, then let's first take ourselves into relatively wild thinking for a while.

Let your imagination run as wild as possible for your dream destination, and wherever you think that you cannot go beyond this point in imagining then hold your thought process.

At this point, start dreaming to feel the happiness of that junction as if you are already there and adopt this position in your mind. Initially, it might be a bit difficult to carry this adopted situation or position, but it is the beginning of a game. As long as you carry this 'Adopted dream child', your confidence will grow because you really want to bring up this child. This confidence should not be your overconfidence or imaginary confidence it should be simply your own, just your own confidence.

There could be a situation where you think that you have adopted something which you cannot carry. It doesn't matter much if you aim for the sky then at least you will get the moon. Unfortunately, if you have adopted something which you find bit bigger than your capacity, then start shredding it off, do not get too much emotionally bonded with your dream child on initial stage, and accommodate as per you capacity of carrying it. So, Good luck and all the best!

You have your own point of view, and there is certainly a basis for the same. Further, they are lined with you and you have some questions to answer.

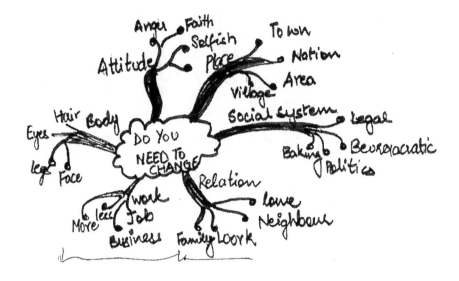

1. Why should you change it?
2. Why can't you improve upon?

If you are confident about your point of view, then you must support the fact that each one of us has a right to have his faith in our own point of view. Express your own views rationally and leave it up to the others to believe it or not. While leaving such an impression over others and while evaluating your confidence level, just observe its effects on the people, try to relate and learn. That's how this angle would help you keeping 'your point of view' in order.

Now gradually start believing that world is really a very simple place to live and success is not a 'so difficult' target to achieve. From here onwards, once you think so, you will start understanding your worth, and respecting yourself because you are thereby amongst those successful people who realized this simple fact of life.

At this point, I highlight an example of 'Newton', the great scientist who discovered the law of gravity. When he saw an apple falling on the ground from a tree, he asked himself, "What made this apple fall on the ground?" He then observed and realized that it is a gravitational force which was applied on the apple which eventually pulled it towards the ground, and then he discovered the law of gravity. It was basically very simple but nobody else realized this phenomenon prior to Newton. Newton discovered it only and passed it on as established and written knowledge.

So, discovering the simplicity is the biggest strength and you have just done it by believing in your point of view.

If your self-respect has started making you think that you are not just a one face in the crowd, then you will stop receiving useless things coming to you. This will be your first step towards the way of your dream goal. This is called **self-respect**. Self-image and feeling happy about oneself are more or less the same.

Your respect in the eyes of your own is the most important qualification to be a successful person. You can maintain and improve your self-respect by adopting few of the following ways:

1. Take care of your health. Follow the rule of "Early to bed early to rise, makes a person healthy wealthy and wise". This proverb has a lot of potential, and by doing so, you will try to finish your work well in time. Most of us keep working and they believe that by working more and more within 24 hours of a day, they can impress others or can get more and more output. This is not completely right. There could be some instances where people got some jumps in their lives, but that is not a rule. I would rather say if we decide to go to bed early, we will surely plan everything and stream line every work in such a way that with appropriate inputs you would get the desired output. You could keep upgrading your work inputs (skills, techniques, quality, excellence, etc.) vertically rather than consuming more time horizontally.
2. After finishing your day's objective or the work you should develop your line of working for the next day, this theory is called

early check and rectification method. It is the best method to be organized and ever recognized by anybody on Earth. If you take your dinner on time you would enjoy it as a food for life, not life for food. This would help you to have healthy body and surely you would take a sound sleep for desired number of hours. When you get up early in the morning, first of all you will have a new confidence of being ahead of other sleepers. You could then go for morning walk, have fresh air, smile to fresh faces, come back and give adequate time to read newspaper, and to care for potted plants if you have at your home. It will help you a lot.

3. Remember, you are not born to keep everybody happy in the world. It is difficult and impossible for any of us to keep everybody happy around us, but we must show regards for their views and gestures. Most of the time people tend to divert in order to become a popular personality in early stage of their life, and people also divert from their objective, role or task of life. They start keeping everybody happy and they always look for compliments. If we do our task well and 'within time', then most of us would naturally become the famous persons. Then you would have a better choice of people in your circle, among them you can satisfy your craving for being popular. Keeping in mind the scenario of today's life, and as per my personal opinion, "It is better to be famous than popular".

4. Think twice before talking to anybody, and sometimes not talking at all may also be good. Most of the people do not think before they talk. When I asked one of my colleagues about it, she said, "I cannot be honest to other person if I always think before I say, and then I will try to say what other person really wants to hear." I didn't agree with her, as it is not appropriate. I think you would rather be more honest if you really think before you speak. Some people think after they speak and then realize that it was not correct. They rectify it by adding few more sentences to their conversation, or they start telling lie one after another. In some cases, if they do not lie, they become adamant on their viewpoint which does not help them in long-run, but for that moment of life they do get the upper hand standpoint and get satisfied by the feeling that what they said was correct.

5. Have a good sense of humor, and enhance or adapt it to match the relevant person. For getting the ideas, read good jokes and enjoy them. You would agree with me that each one of us wants to enjoy and smile. If you use right type of sense of humor, you

will have a natural confidence in you and people will regard you for your wit. Wit comes with your open-minded gesture.

Beware! Your extra sense of humor might drift you towards feeling over-smartness. Over-smartness might lead you towards extra witty person, and which in sequence might lead you to be sarcastic and sarcasm further might lead you to be a ridiculer person. Do not grow your humor power as your enemy. **So, just be careful about it!**

---

6. Just do not visit, enter or barge in everywhere because all places are not made for you. Most of the people join or visit everywhere. It is not so bad or harmful, but it does effects your image in your own eyes prior to someone else. It makes more sense if we visit anywhere gracefully, enjoy whole-heartedly, come back respectfully, leave behind a door open for the next time and invite them humbly to one's place.

7. You should acknowledge a fact that you have your own set of strengths and weaknesses. Nobody on this earth is flawless. You are among them only, and with this combination of strengths and weaknesses you are going to be a successful person. You should not compare yourself with everybody around us because whatever qualities you have—others might not, and whatever qualities others have—you might not have. By accepting this, you would have better self-respect. Maintain you dignity. Each and every tiny little thing in the world has its own worth for the system. In other words, you should have a positive quality of taking the inspiration from any good source for improving your life. **The concept of taking the inspirations 'positively' is totally different from an act of making unhealthy comparisons with others.** This may help you to become a better person in life. It is you who has to realize first, rather than waiting for someone else to make you realize.

8. **Be a human of words**, it will enhance your image in your own eyes. You should regard and fulfill your own words, promises and commitments. It could be any matter such as:

   • If you say to someone, "I will come to your party," then be there as scheduled.
   • If you say, "I will take care," then do take care.

- If you say, "I will pay you 'x . . .' amount," then do pay it on time.
- When you say, "I will not do this . . . ," then stick to it.

Any unforeseen deviance from your statement, promise or commitment due to genuine reasons or unavoidable circumstances must be sincerely and timely communicated for the convenience of concerned person. If you follow such things, it will enhance your self-respect.

Beware! Too much of self-respect also drifts a person towards arrogance. Whereby arrogance leads to stubbornness, which further leads to argumentativeness, and argumentativeness finally leads to frustration. **So, just be careful about it**

---

3. Should have a Dream—If you lack

Before we proceed, it should be understood that there is a hairline difference between dream and vision. Most of us believe that dream is a vision. In my views, "Dream is our desire, whereas vision is a systematic thought process to reach it. It includes the planning part and 'its' step by step proceedings. Our dreams are more like fantasies, but making these fantasies into a real story is a vision."

Most of the successful people in this World had a dream. Mahatma Gandhi wanted to see India as an independent country. Mr Dhirubhai Ambani wanted to become the owner of a company in which he used to work as a helper. Wright Brothers wanted to fly. You can find various such examples in your Nation. It is natural and quite obvious that each one of us usually have a dream, such as, a dream to achieve something in our life, be it—to become a top most scholar or a big businessman or the Chief of Army staff, or to have an adorable house wife. It all depends upon our likenesses and the impressions we carry about ourselves. As stated in previous topic, self-respect is the foremost factor for our lives. It will automatically create a dream for us. Everything is inter-related. Aim for "Castle in the air" and start putting foundation under it and you will find one day that you own this castle, or dream for sky you will at least get the moon. Without a dream in your life, you would **not be able to develop and nurture your power of vision** which is the subsequent step of being a successful person.

When I worked for a small-scale industry as helper making electronic regulators, I used to dream that one day I must have a big cloth mill with my initial name RK written on it, I was very young (just 14 years of age) at that time. When I shared this dream with my neighbors, they asked me, "Do you know it would require lots of money to build it?" I answered, "So what, people themselves will invest in my company because I am going to give them good cloth to wear," and my neighbors used to laugh at me. However, I could not become a cloth mill owner till now, but I have professionally reached to a decent position where I am a CEO of mid-sized company manufacturing and selling Ayurvedic tooth powder/paste and herbal products. As of now, several people are our Distributors, Agents, and these people have also invested in our stocks and deposits, and that too without any written agreement. As we want them to believe our words, and so we are sincerely committed to them. I strongly believe that the committed words have much more value than a written agreement. I always tell my peer group that business is done on words, and court cases on written material.

Within few years at the age of 17, I dreamt of becoming a national level personality by the time I reach of 35 years of age. I wanted to see my photograph at front page of "Business Today", a leading business magazine in India, but I was not sure about "what to do" so as to become a personality of that stature. However, I started formulating 5 Year plans that by the age of 25 years I should be at a Branch Manager level, by next 5 years I would promote a company, and at the end of second 5 year lap I will take this company up to a National repute level. It was my entire dream. What I was lacking in this was the vision, which I further realized at an age of 27 (after passing 10 years).

If I had found a Guru or a 'Blue Book' of this kind as a help and guidance at the time when I dreamt it (as above), then it would have been much useful to me for having a step by step approach to achieve my dreams. I would have surely become a National level personality by the time of 35 years of my age. But this is what we can call a destiny or a poor vision. It was only a dream. I did not get a miraculous Guru sort of person, but circumstances and various situations taught me to think in the better direction. Although I am lagging behind the schedule of my dream by 9 years as of 2011, but I don't worry as I know that I am on the right track.

Our dream need not necessarily come true, but having one is very important. The sooner it is the better it is, because our inputs, our planning and our destiny will help us to go towards it. Believe me, it is true! Therefore one must have a dream to fulfill, followed by a vision.

Beware! Over-dreaming also drifts a person towards fool's paradise, which further leads to confusions, and confusions will not lead you anywhere. **So, just be careful about it!**

---

4. Develop a vision—If you lack

(on one side you got ballooning thoughts intermingled but meaning ful—on other side you need to make it categorical)

After understanding the topics like: "Know your present status", "Have self-respect" and "Should have a dream", now the 4th Step goes on to **'vision'**. At this step, you should start converting your wild imagination into a vision. Vision can be developed by observing the surroundings, by collecting the lessons into your basket which you get from your day to day life, current affairs, relations, friends, nature and history. You should develop or must have the curiosity. Your curiosity will lead to a question, your search for the answer will develop your mind-power, and your mind-power will strengthen your vision apart from adding new points into your mind-basket. Just realize that, you can develop your strengths to achieve the goals while filling your mind-basket with new lessons. This is going to be amazing!

"Forethoughtfulness of our mind is also called vision."

Reverse planning (from end to the present), thinking on the possible hurdles and diversions, preparing your mind to solve and overcome them are the parts of a vision. Let me put it in a bit simpler manner. Your parents had a vision to get you admitted in such a school where you studied for 12 years to make your future bright. They searched for a good school, compared it with other schools in the city, asked a few people about it, and then got you admitted in class 1ˢᵗ or may be in kindergarten. Similarly, we must think about our future at least for next 10 years and keep shaping our daily, monthly and yearly tasks so that we can possibly remain on the right track which we opted as our dream.

"Making principles to guide or lead one's life is also called a vision." Most of the people live their life without self-discipline which harms them in the long-run. Vision is the same thing which makes us feels proud of ourselves. It is better to understand hunger beforehand and then go for hunting, rather than just to go for a hunt to get anything you lay your hands on. I believe once your inner power is awaken up by you, you can get a better and clearer vision. This power would further help you making your path firmer.

In the year 1991, when I asked a person during one of the interviews for a managerial post, "Where do you see yourself 3 years from now?"

He smiled at me and said, "Sir, at your position."

Then I asked, "What does it mean?"

He said humbly, "Sir I would like to rise up to your position and would be taking someone else's interview like this, as a selection authority."

I told him, "It seems that you are impressed by my position."

He replied, "Yes".

I asked, "Do you think, my job is to interview the candidates?"

He said, "No".

I asked, "Then what do you think my job is?"

He replied, "Sir, I am not sure about it."

I told this young man, "See you are not sure about exact nature of my job, but you are impressed by my position. Don't you think that your vision is actually not clear! It is rather a fallacy!"

He felt shy and said, "Sorry Sir."

I told him, "You need not to be sorry for it. Do not try to please me by saying sorry, you are here to catch hold of an opportunity which is suitable for you, and this suitability will be gauged by both of us. So, be what you are."

He said, "Sir I was thinking it to be a rosy and impressing position and could flatter you with this answer."

I replied, "Yes, I think now you are right, as you have expressed your real inner-self. Now tell me, where you would like to see yourself after 3 years from now."

And he had no answer . . . !

However, he had some more relevant valuable points to be selected, and on those grounds he was through. But most of us live in the impression mode rather than living in the visionary mode. It is your vision which takes you there not the hit and trial method. Hit and trial can be opted when you are going out of your way to help someone or to attempt something new, not in your main course of life.

Each one of us is a **visionary**. The differences among people are about their different thinking capabilities with respect to visualizing the future distances from the present moment.

People those who have a **vision** of 25 years ahead of the present, may become successful scientists.

People those who have a **vision** of 10 years ahead of the present, may become successful businessmen.

People those who have a **vision** of 5 years ahead of the present, may become successful entrepreneurs.

People those who have a **vision** of 2 years ahead of the present, may become good servicemen.

People those who have a **vision** between the present to 2 years ahead, are heading the society and the masses.

People those who have **no vision** and they have only the present to think of, may somehow manage to survive. They 'just follow' others as they are like sheep. They suffer a lot in the long-run.

There are two types of changes which occur in the society one is sluggish and the other one is quick. If we watch society as an observer we will notice both of them, and if we can recall or refer the past experience of the "task" in question, we can develop our **vision**.

My present is good, my past was nice and my future will be wonderful. People bearing such a thought have very good vision because they live their life without any regret. Whatever has happened, it always happens for the good, and whatever is going to happen will happen for good. This is another very spiritual and strong point of view to have a great vision, because after having this thought only you can freely imagine and freely run your mind to draw the best possible line of action for the future, considering all pros and cons of your life.

(Gautam Buddha)

Here I give an example of Gautam Buddha. He sat under a tree and started running his mind which led him to a question and by simply meditating he started getting the answer, each answer led him to the next question and then its relevant answer. At the end of process, he got *Brahmagyan* (the ultimate knowledge of bliss). People started believing him and became his followers. His observations during his princely life and his basic studies were the only thing with him as his Guru, and he became Lord Gautam Buddha. Today there are millions of people in the world who believe in him and his religion. Lord Gautam Buddha was a great visionary of the past centuries. His aim was different but the method was more or less the same which is required by all of us to attain success and bliss.

Another way to have a vision . . .

When you were young, you believed that this world has lots of things to give you. Yes, up to some extent you were correct. Do you know you have received or acquired just 1% of it till now, and rest of 99% will come to you in the due course of your life? To receive anything, you must have a basket with you to receive anything. If you do not keep a basket with you, you would not be able to receive and carry anything along. You should make your own basket or prepare yourself to make a basket. This basket is nothing but your own mind. If your mind has a positive attitude and you belief in truthfulness, then your half of the job is done with it only. Rest 50% of the job would be done during your course of receiving good things with the positive attitude. Initially you may find most of the things useless because you are not able to put a tangible value to them. Be careful that they might seem useless to you initially, but further whenever you would apply those good points in real life situations, you will realize the importance of those things which you picked up in your past.

You might have few questions in mind while studying in school that why do you have to learn history, civics or craft like subjects? How are these going to help you? Probably you often wanted to omit these subjects from the course. You used to think it because at that point of time you were not able to put tangible value to it, and there were no direct applications of these subjects in your life at that point of time. But later, you might have realized the real value of these subjects. Similarly there are various things in our life (when faced upfront), we cannot attach tangible value to them, but it does not mean that they have no value. Therefore, filling your basket with those learning is not futile but it is fruitful. It can be observed that each and everything in the universe has its worth which is directly or indirectly related to you or the life whether at a 'micro' or 'macro' level.

BEWARE! Excessive visionary attitude drifts a person towards fairy tales, which further leads to new fairy tales and it lead a person to be emotional. Finally emotional attitude does not allow you to take professional steps. **So, just be careful about it!**

---

5. Gain confidence—If you are under-confident

Let's move further and recall your dreams, its benefits and the happiness you felt at one point of time. This time is to recollect your **confidence**, as it is going to help you move ahead. To the inspiration, I bring into focus a well known story of "The Thirsty Crow".

Crow was confident that water would come up to drinking level and he believed in his strengths. He picked up several pebbles one by one and kept putting them in the pot. Finally he succeeded, the water-level came up and he drank the water. His motive was to drink water and he was confident that after putting lots of pebbles, the water level would come up and he would drink it.

Its story can be used as an inspiration.

For you, it is the beginning of the show of success now. This can be done only if you are confident. Just be confident, but not be over-confident!

It is very important for anybody to really understand the hairline difference between the Confidence and Overconfidence.

Confidence is our best friend, but overconfidence is our worst enemy. Generally it becomes difficult for us to understand the difference. To make it simpler, I elaborate it with an example: "It can be said as a **confidence** when you feel comfortable and cool to manage any circumstance with your capabilities," on the contrary, "It can be said as a **overconfidence** in any circumstance when you feel excited and proud of your inner power and capabilities that you will win. It is also the careless or miscalculated exaggeration of own capabilities in one's mind." As a matter of fact, it is just nothing for me, but it must be considered that, if one has a careless attitude to deal with the circumstance having assumption of winning is called overconfidence. So we should remain cool, calm and modest while evaluating ourselves. We should also be careful to put in our optimum efforts for achieving victory, and should actually express the feeling of triumph only after getting the victory. This may help us to be even more confident. We can begin the task with a statement **"I think I can do it, let me try."**

Before or while performing a job (no matter how fresh or repetitive it is), rethink about it with a fresh point of view, and process all pros and cons meticulously. Be careful about it, as it may be beneficial for you to have a fresh faith in your confidence every time you do your task.

BEWARE! Non-renewed confidence drifts a person towards overconfidence. Whereby, overconfidence leads a person to high self-expectation, which further leads to short cuts, and short cuts might meet dead end. **So, just be careful about it!**

---

6. Just work hard—If you are a lazy person

(This passage is suggested to be read thrice)

Each one of us (be it a kid, a youngster or a fully grown-up person) has few basic similarities, such as, operating limbs, survival strength and desire to live. We all work up to some extent, and this working capacity varies from person to person. Few people work a bit more than others because their need is more than others. Few people work even harder because they want to achieve much more than others. Quantum of work done by the people has direct relation to their needs and ambitions.

When it comes to fulfill our needs, we have to work hard so as to keep growing with the natural pace of life. Hard work is just the answer to it. We have a latent energy in us, and it is to be kindled up by the hard work so that it can be converted into talent. There is no substitute of hard work. It means we have no other option to choose, as we cannot skip hard work to reach our goal, for example, if an athlete has to run 100 meters race to win, he will have to run several kilometers daily to build his stamina so that he can utilize his entire stamina in the competition, of just 100 meters race.

The appropriate inputs are required to be put into action regularly in the form of hard work to finally get the desired results. Hard work cannot be compromised due to lack of "anything", such as, money or inappropriate surroundings.

Hard work can be defined in many ways:

- Consistency in performing the routine work is hard work.
- Working with focus on the task is hard work.
- Not resting till the job is done is hard work.
- Falling and getting-up to restart is hard work.
- Accepting the challenge and working towards it, is hard work.

We should work hard because we are capable of it, and not because someone has told us to work hard. Our inner zeal is more important factor than someone else's motivating lecturer. Motivational lectures are good for providing initiative to work, but it is our inner zeal which drives us ahead by keeping such initiative alive is also called hard work.

Once again I would like to draw your attention on the story of "The thirsty crow". He was a very hard working bird. He kept on putting pebbles in the pot until water came up to a drinking level. "Just imagine . . . ! How much quantity of water could up each time when he dropped a single stone in the pot?" Each and every time he could manage to drop just a single stone only and he continued his efforts, this is called hard work.

So let's get an inspiration from such a story to put in our best efforts to the "pot of life", and we will see one day that water would be there for us at a drinking level.

Recall the story of—Tortise and Rabit—when rabit was lazy and tortoise hard working with consistency and he won the race.

Here I repeat hard work in a nutshell. It is an age-old saying that there is no substitute of hard work. We should remember that one has to work hard whether a person does any highly intellectual work or the menial work. If we give our best then best will come back to us in all respective domains.

We would not be called a hard worker if:

- We do the work with an "expectation" or to get its "guaranteed output", in such a case our mind is not working towards the job but it is working towards the desire and waiting for the output to come. Therefore, the inner enemy called desire dominates us.
- We work on the condition of getting the desired output beforehand without putting appropriate inputs, then such a course of action towards it cannot be counted as a hard work, but it would just be called simply a normal work.

It should be noted that, working with a motivation when combined with hard work increases the chances of attaining success.

We all know, it is tough but it is necessary for us to simultaneously defeat our inner enemies, such as, impatience, indiscipline, carelessness or desires that deviate us from doing hard work. Work hard as much as required. Do not be inconsistent until the task is finished, then see what comes back as a reward. One must work hard due to one's own dignity and capabilities of doing it, but not because one is told to do hard work.

It must be agreed upon that our hard work will gradually shape into smart work. **It is very important to realize that appropriate amount of hard work should be poured in, and not an excessive amount.** It is the law of life that suitable inputs get us the maximum output. Inputs should be so refined and precise that it could lead to the outcome of success.

BEWARE! Too much of hard work drifts a person towards donkey's attitude. Whereby, donkey's attitude risks a person to be exploited by others. Such exploitation will not let oneself to get explored and it will rather consume one's work power totally. **So, just be careful about it!**

---

7. Confrontation is a part of life—
Don't feel shy to do so

Each one us in life experience several situations into which we might not feel comfortable or satisfied. I have seen several people in life who wear an attitude of "Let it go . . . ," or do compromise or remain inactive on the objectionable issue. It does not seem to be correct if a person avoid confrontation with other person's irrational, unethical behavior and acts, especially when it is causing trouble to him or to others. Therefore, confrontation may be a good option to act upon for making the things straight. A decent confrontation is a positive gesture! At least . . . , the reaction or answer of the concerned person will help you to access the situation in a better way. To say, "I felt bad . . . !" is a confrontation, rather than saying "I oppose this act . . ." in a rude way. Voting against an unacceptable deed is confrontation. We should gracefully maintain the decorum and self-respect, while being into confrontation with others. Insulting others or passing the comments sarcastically is not a confrontation. **We must follow the right method to deal with the wrong person.**

It is a confrontation when you say directly to the concerned person about its unacceptable behavior or act. When you say so . . . , then most of times the other person either rectifies it or offers an apology admitting his mistake or he puts his point of view to convince and satisfy you. About eighty percent of the people may take it in a healthy way, and those twenty percent people who don't rationalize themselves would automatically prove themselves to be duffers, arrogant, short-sighted or ignorant in their lives.

There are still so many good people in the world. I would say majority of people are basically good, and that is why the World is growing and developing. Whereas, most of us think that the World has gone mad and it is full of selfish and bad people now. The circumstances actually make a person to drop down from good to bad. Good remains good and deviant person may soon rectify or take control over his adverse circumstance, and may recover as a good person. On the contrary, few fundamentally bad people may remain bad or even they become worse. As a matter of fact, it is up to us to confront and help them to grow because after all we have some human grounds in our mind.

One should confront not to take revenge but to develop the society for tomorrow. It is the other person, you and your coming generation who would live in this society and the World. So, by confrontation you would actually rectifying the wrong and making the future bright for yourself and others.

A lot of courage is required to confront with the unjust activities of others. One can get the courage by the virtue of one's own strengths, qualities, self-discipline, self-respect, vision and the hard work done, as mentioned in previous pages.

Once I was scheduled to fly from Delhi to Ahmadabad. My air ticket was in waiting list, and I was in a queue at 4th position. Suddenly a person came rushing and pushed his hand through the reservation window out of turn, and started asking about the confirmation of his ticket. He seemed to be a rich and educated person. No one made any objection, but I could not stop myself, and I tapped his shoulder to ask him, "Gentleman, why don't you come in the queue?" He replied arrogantly, "I am asking for 1st Class reservation status." Then my next Question to him was, "What do you think I was trying for . . . ?"

Just having asked such a question, this guy felt ashamed and coolly stood behind me. I then said, "I felt bad that is why I confronted you for your action." He felt sorry and said, "He was worried and in panic whether he would get his seat confirmed or not."

However, fortunately all of us standing in the queue got the tickets confirmed. Later on, the same guy not only became my fellow passenger but also a friend.

When the confrontation is resolved, we must politely suggest our opinion about the sensible or ideal course of action or behavior (which could have followed by the other person), the lack of which actually caused the confrontation. In this way s/he would be introduced to another way of doing it. Or (at least . . . ,) we would also get the satisfaction of expressing our point of view. **It is not always necessary that our point of view is better than that of other person with whom we confronted.** Even we could also get some of our myths cleared in this course of interaction!

BEWARE! Too much of confrontation habit might drift a person towards nagging. Whereby, nagging may force a person towards disappointment, which further necessitates a person to understand the facts. **So, just be careful to understand the facts and system!**

---

8. Happiness is the key word—If you are sad or does not frequently feel happy

Happiness: It is a state of mind. Happiness may be materialistic, non-material or may involve both of them. It may be emotional, physical, or something else which cannot be defined in words . . . ! It is an experience which can only be experienced, and it is beyond explanation. We can try to be happy into whatever the situations we face in life. It is an invisible fuel which always helps us to be on the road to success. Whatever we do in life . . . , we should try to do it with happiness. In case if we succeed, then our happiness would get multiplied. Or, God forbid that if we lose, then also we gain because we have already gained the happiness of performing the task. At last, it is only the happiness for which we all are living for . . . !

Long back, it was about 7 p.m in Nov 1986. when I returned to office from my daily sales schedule. I was quite depressed and tired because I could not meet target Sales for that day. I was then working as a door to door salesman of a house cleaning machine. When I came back to office, as usual I saw my boss (Mr. H.K. Singha, who used to stay in the same building where my office was situated.)

He asked me, "Hi champ, how was the day?"

I said, "It was very boring, tiring and unproductive."

Then he asked, "Did you enjoy making calls?"

I replied, "What enjoyment . . . , Sir? Since morning I was under pressure to sell at least one unit today, because I could not sale even a single machine since past 5 days, despite my hard work."

He said, "Rohit, it is just 8 p.m. now, let's go to the field once again."

I asked him, "Now . . . Isn't it too late?"

He said, "So what . . . ? People have not gone to sleep yet, they usually sleep at 10 p.m., let's go."

He took his motorbike and asked me to sit behind, and I sat with a demo kit on my lap on the pillion seat. While going for the cold call again my Boss sang a Hindi song and I played its rhythm on my demo kit. I then felt as relaxed and fresh as it feels in the morning hours. We made a cold call in one of the premium residential area in the city. This time my boss made the call and I just watched his cool patience, enthusiasm and confidence. It took us about one & a half hour to finish the demo and the sales call. At the end, we could not sell it to that customer. We packed our demo kit and came back to office. My Boss said, "Never mind Rohit, tomorrow again we'll go for fresh calls together." I returned home neither sad nor depressed and without success, but still I had a good sleep that night. Next day at 10.30 a.m. my boss received a telephonic call from someone, and he called me in his room. He told me to get a new machine issued in my name and deliver it to the same person whom we gave the demo last night. This man wanted to purchase the machine for his daughter living in some other State (where our sales office was not started till then). I was thrilled as I not only got the sale but also the new happiness to work for that day. It really pays to be happy, but we never know when . . . !

Let me elaborate the happiness step by step:

Question No.1. What is Happiness?

Answer: Satisfaction is Happiness.

Question No.2. What is satisfaction?

Answer: Gratification is satisfaction.

Question No.3. How to get gratification?

Answer: Total devotion to the subject will give gratification.

Question No.4. How to give total devotion?

Answer: Work done with full truthfulness is devotion.

Question No.5. What is full truthfulness?

Answer: Such an attitude when the act is performed keeping in mind that it is not harming me or others, directly or indirectly.

Question No.6. What is the general meaning of attitude and harm in above answer?

Answer: Attitude means you inner notion, and harm means any type of loss.

Question No.7. How to build the positive harmless attitude?

Answer: With love . . . , which itself means respect.

Respect means sense of belonging.

Sense of belonging means one's inclination towards the subject.

Inclination means one's caring attitude.

Care means one's protection.

Protection means one's belief.

Belief means one's confidence.

Confidence means one's devotion.

Devotion means one's inner power.

Inner power means *Panchbhoot (Jal, Vayu, Aakash, Agni & Prithvi)*

Panchbhoot itself means the God.

God means the truth.

Truth comes with devotion.

Devotion means gratification.

Gratification means satisfaction.

Satisfaction means happiness.

Happiness means Bliss.

Bliss means Moksha.

Moksha means getting dissolved in supernatural power.

Getting dissolved means getting spread all over along with the supernatural power.

Supernatural means *Panchbhoot*.

Panchbhoot means *Parampita Parmeshwar* or the God.

Therefore, God is the ultimate happiness. To be happy, be with God and be natural!

(Try to re-read and re-understand last 23 lines)

9. Faith—nothing has 'worth' without it— If you have lost it

(I am about to reach to Oasis)

You must have faith in yourself, and faith in your job, in your luck, inputs, support system, seniors and juniors. Above all, you must have a faith in God. Living or working without faith is something like a sea without fish, a human body without blood, a jungle without animals, a food without taste, a school without books, and a sports man without stamina. On the basis of faith you would feel happy, satisfied, grown up and confident. You would have no regrets!

Here I share a small incidence about an attitude and faith of a person who is very closely associated with my life. Once he told me that in the city of Jaipur, there is a temple of Lord Ganesha located up on a hill.

He was told by few devotees who are my friends too that, "A person can get his wish fulfilled by visiting 'bare feet' to this temple regularly for 11 Wednesdays."

I asked him, "Did you follow this ritual?"

He said, "Yes . . . , I went there for 11 Wednesdays religiously, but nothing happened as desired by me."

Then I asked, "So what happed after that?"

He said, "I have lost my deep faith in that temple."

In the above incidence, I think this person did not have any faith in his wish. He just thought that his wish could be fulfilled just by walking bare feet to a temple. I think that he just performed only the ritual of walking up to the hill physically, but did not work religiously on the task. Such types of rituals are prescribed to be performed for such a long period consistently, so that the faith of a person in his wish and the pouring in capacity of the inputs in his task does not drift. One could achieve the desired goal through perseverance, and not by just walking up and down to any hill Temple or Mosque or Church. Temples, Mosques or Churches are not the places where God lives. These are the places of worship. God lives everywhere. **First of all, God is there within us in the form of the spiritual essence of all the Truth, Faith, Positive energies, Good Qualities and the Life force.** It is also a fact that various places of worship have their worth in terms of religious strength.

Faith in a deity might be supportive if it is merged with the perseverance and power of one's own Karma (the action), and if it is followed along with observing the truth of an old saying, "God help those who help themselves."

Faith is not an outside factor. It is deep inside one's heart and mind. It is most important that faith should be there within oneself that one would religiously perform the task until the goal is achieved. God definitely helps those who really help themselves, but God would not help those who try to lure him by performing just the physical act of worship only. Worship has definitely a vital role to play but at the later stage. It is the faith which matters prior to worship. It reminds me of the year mid-1999, when I made the first few sales calls to search for a dealer/ stockiest for my own product "YDM-Yunadent" which is herbal toothpowder for dental problems. It is an excellent dental cleanser and polisher too. I visited 2-3 businessmen in the market with an offer to get them appointed as our Sales Distributor. They were not interested to become one because of the simple reason that there was no demand for our new product in the market. I had just 17 shops in hand from where my father used to sell "Yunadent" products on consignment basis (which means to get paid after the product is sold).

Once I was making the last call of the day and I told to our prospect that, "I have always been successful in my service tenure, and I strongly hope that our product would one day become one of the successful products in the State, no matter how small a quantity we are selling today. Every new product and concept in the world always gets started by 1 person or a unit, and later on it gets zeros added to their right side. I have a tremendous faith in myself, my work and moreover I had no choices to make for my future."

This man said, "Ok! I would become your Sales Distributor, but I would buy only 128 units for now (which meant two box packs)."

I said, "It is fine and thanks to your judgment, I assure that you would always be happy for this decision."

This order was worth Rs 700 only, but I felt it to be equivalent to Rs 7000 and may be more. While returning home I visited a temple and offered *"Prasad"* worth Rs 11 and shared it with my father at home, he was happy and blessed me for success. With the grace of God in year 2011 (as of now) the same Sales Distributor is selling the same product of worth more than Rs 5,00,000 per month with full confidence and faith, that too without any efforts.

It was the faith of Sales Distributor, my own faith and God's blessing on us, which led all the way to this day. Remember! Every mass is made of several molecules, and one should have faith in each and every molecule.

BEWARE! Blind faith might drift a person towards adopting a biased attitude, which further forces a person to do several unwanted, intangible and hypothetical acts. So, a blind faith may not lead him anywhere.

---

10. Developing Devotion—If you lack

Devotion: It is co-related with faith (the previous topic). Where you have faith the essence will follow in the form of devotion, and devotion is nothing but the dedication, focus. It is the inner support of the faith. Devotion would find dedication which would give direction. The elements of **d**evotion, **d**edication and **d**irection together comprise a 3-D formula of success.

Once when a person focuses on the task then things begin to sail very smoothly. To achieve devotion . . . , one should just forget about all the irrelevant and unimportant matters. One should just leave the senses behind and concentrate over the work to achieve the goal, and leave the rest to Almighty God. Then just get yourself mentally inside a cocoon that is very comforting and safe which is called God's coupe or lap, and enjoy God's love, blessings and safety. He takes care of you.

Let's further observe the development of devotion. Who can develop devotion? Believe me . . . ! I have come across several people, especially those who are in a hurry to reach the top or to be successful very soon or at their early stage of life. Such people have Soda water bottle like enthusiasm which goes up very fast and comes down with the same speed. Their devotion is generally short-lived and they lose hope very soon. Developing faith in the goal is very important for anybody from any walk of life.

Each one of us must do our best and believe that whatever we are doing is in fact one of the best tasks ever performed in the world, and the world is incomplete without such a task. A person would tend to be more devoted towards the work by having such an attitude. If billions of people can have billions of unique fingerprints within the same 1 square inch of fingertip, and each snowflake dropped on Earth is unlike others (which are also trillions in count within an hour), then why can't we look at different aspects of our lives with few different perspectives so as to explore something new each time, which might further get us devoted with a new zeal every time. A fresh look into the subject every time enhances person's devotional power. It may sound difficult but it is possible!

Let's clarify the above concept with more practical examples:

a) Whenever you drive a vehicle, you drive it through traffic with a new degree of alertness each time because it might be difficult to ascertain about the type and direction of vehicles or the traffic which comes across, or the unpredictable accidents that may occur.
b) Whenever you play any game, you adopt a new strategy, or think of new ideas to act and respond each time because it may be very difficult to ascertain the opponent's next action or reaction.
c) Whenever you fly a kite, you think of new ideas and perform various actions to fly it each time because of the changing direction of unpredictable wind, and you never know about the directions from where your other flying mates may give you a chase. It keeps the development of your devotion alive and active.

Hope . . . , the importance of adopting a fresh perception is clarified here! In all the above circumstances, you keep your devotion alive because you have a fear of loss which is tangible. If it was not tangible, you might have deteriorated in your devotion. Consider all that is happing around you as tangible. Time and duration of response may vary when you understand its tangible value.

11. Facing the failure—If you have failed

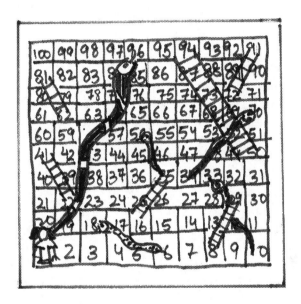

(recall your child hood game snakes and ladders)

Adhering to all above points (as mentioned in previous pages) does not ensure success, due to various factors that could be directly or indirectly related to you, and so you could still fail in spite of following all the above steps. The failure causing factors could include any of the "other reasons", such as, your support system, desires, time factor, resources or it could be your sheer destiny (luck). You have no control over your failure. I have come across several people who keep trying until success is attained. As a matter of fact, they are such people who fear failure, never gave high value to the defeats and falls which came to their way to success. It is also one of the ways to take the life. Being a failure, might be a new opportunity on the road of success in a different manner. So don't be disheartened because of failure. Have courage to restart, it is never late than "never"!

It was October 1985 when I had a call letter from Indian Air Force (IAF) to appear for practical test for joining there as the Flying Officer. It was a direct entry after my NCC—'C' Certificate exams which I passed successfully. I had few hours of flying experience including Solo flying. I was a fine pupil pilot, and my landing skill was admired by one and all, especially my instructor (Wing Commander Khanna) who was also a Wing Commander-cum-private pilot appointed for the Chief Minister of Rajasthan at that time. These facts used to give me lot of confidence which later on turned into my overconfidence.

When I received this call letter, I was thrilled and conveyed about it to all my friends, "Now I have received the call letter and I would be joining IAF." It was a matter of passing just two tests, namely, Pilot Aptitude Battery Test (PABT) and Drum test. I concentrated on my flying chapter and theory before going to Dehra Dun for the test. Everybody used to tell my mother that, "Your son is a very good flyer, and he is sure to become a pilot from this batch of NCC." My mother used to feel proud of me and so did I. I can still clearly recall, it was morning session around 8.30 a.m. when we all were called for the test briefing before we appeared for the exam. Exam started at about 9 a.m. The first was PABT Screen test, and I secured 90% marks in it. My invigilator told me, "You have really scored very high. Well done!" He further asked me, "Are you a flyer?" I proudly said, "Yes." At that point of time my enthusiasm was further heightened and confidence swelled more. Then, second test was the Drum test. It was the rudest of shocks as I could not perform in it at all. As a matter of fact, none of my flying instructors ever gave me an idea about this test, I still do not know why? It was really like a nightmare.

Then the time came for announcement of result. The Commanding Officer came and said, "I am going to call the names of those candidates who will not continue in this race." He started calling out names one by one. When it gradually approached towards the alphabet of my name, my heart started beating at a rate of over 150 beats per minute, and I started sweating. When he called even my name, then my eyes refused to blink as if I had lost my ground control forever, then I left the room and the city without saying a word to anybody including myself. I was zapped!

While coming back to Jaipur, I kept thinking about the past three years of my flying experience, expectations of people and my mother. My future stared at me, "What am I going to do now in my life?" I never had an affinity with civil culture, I never had a good friend circle, I always wanted to become a fighter pilot, but what could be done next . . . , then? I was worried about my very uncertain future at that time. At last, when I came back and shared this bad news with my mother, then she consoled me and said, "God wanted you to be with me, and not with IAF." That very simple sentence from her made me forget everything, and I got a new zeal to face the future.

Since I was just a Commerce Graduate, I chose a simple job of a salesman in the city, and started working with the same zeal which I used to carry as pupil pilot. Everything went well, today I have no regrets about anything I did or whatsoever happened with me. I always thank God for helping me to face my failure and to build a new future.

12. Crisis Management—If you are in a crisis

After the failure . . . , the stage of Crisis follows. We must know how to face and deal with the crises. Crisis is the most horrible war for each one of us indeed. We often use this word in our day-to-day life.

Let's understand about Crisis:

- ❖ What is meant by Crisis?
  Crisis can simply be understood as a situation when a person cannot think what to do next . . . !
- ❖ How many types of Crises are there?
  There is only one type of Crisis, and it is man-made. Mind you! Yes, it is the person who creates the Crisis, or responsible for it directly or indirectly.
- ❖ How to face and deal with the Crisis?
  The most important part of Crisis is about, how to handle it step by step. Before discussing the ideas about management of crisis, let's understand that, "What is similar to the Crisis in nature?"

Answer is fire. Yes, Crises are very similar to "fire". When fire occurs, we tend to panic, shout. We immediately rush for any possible help or the item to extinguish fire—be it water, sand or blanket. Else we try to run away without identifying the cause or "type" of fire. There may be several types of fires, such as, short circuit, flame in oil, burning of stocks or wood material, blast and fire, fire due to inflammable gases. Each type of fire requires a different method to extinguish it.

Now let's discuss about the management of crises. Great Challenges in life are also handled in similar way.

Dos:

1. First of all, just watch for a while and observe the situation without panic.
2. Contemplate with a cool mind about the cause of Crisis, and try to prevent or rectify the cause with positive and creative ideas.
3. Collect your resources and share the Crisis situation with your seniors or the experts for their help.
4. Create a distance from the situation. Try not to be trapped like a victim even if you are already victimized. Try to mange it for a while on your own and then ask for suitable help.
5. Another way to deal with the Crisis is to deviate from its effect (problematic part) for a short period, and try to plan a modus operandi to destroy its root cause ethically and legally.

Don'ts:

(Generally most of us do it)

1. Do not mess the situation further by trying to solve it immediately.
2. Do not expect help from everyone.
3. Do not hide it from everyone.
4. Do not react to the situation by getting angry or expressing frustration, irritation in order to satisfy the ego (self-image).
5. One should evaluate the truth of a situation properly. He should have the courage to accept one's own responsibility (if any) sincerely for the cause of Crisis, and should not blame someone else to be responsible for it. It is one's own internal (moral) weakness to unethically pass on the blame to someone else who is innocent. Do not ever say, "Why it has happened to me only, and not to others?"
6. Do not consider it to be the "end" of life. It is just a "bend" in life.

You should always keep one shoulder in your life to cry upon and two feet to touch, and then your vision, karma and God would take care of everything.

I further give an example of a Crossword game:

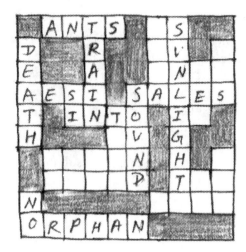

CROSS WORD

To solve the crossword puzzle, it is important to keep the clarity of question in mind and then search for an appropriate word. It is not necessary to fill in the crossword questions in a strict sequence or the order such as, solving question No.1 first of all, then No.2, then No.3 and so on . . . . It is possible that one can solve the puzzle questions in any sequence, such as, solving the question No.3 first (suppose horizontally), then question No.5 (suppose vertically) and suddenly finds the answer to question No.1, then continues to solve several other questions. Then the player may get stuck at the last two questions, again suddenly, at this point, the player generally asks for the help to family members or friends who are not "actually involved" into solving the puzzle, but still they may give some clues to help him get one answer. In spite of help, one question may still be left incomplete. Then a player either quits the crossword or discontinues it temporarily at such point of time. Later on after 1-2 hours, the answer may click to player's mind, and he finally fills it to complete the puzzle. Actually it gives satisfaction to a player for solving the puzzle himself, and unless he does it on his own, he does not get the satisfaction of playing. Player knows that after filling the crossword, he would neither get recognized as a champion and nor he would get any reward, but still he does it for satisfaction because he thinks that he is capable of solving it.

Similarly the Crises management may be somewhat like the concept of solving the crossword puzzle in an indefinite sequence.

My "own life's" Episode on Crises management:

It was September 1997 when I came back to Jaipur after leaving my job where I was working as a National level Manager in India's one of the top most company and drawing a monthly salary of Rs 30,000 which is almost equivalent to now's (year 2011) monthly salary of Rs 3,00,000 or (6500 USD). It was a sufficient amount of money to maintain a decent living standard at that time. I decided to shift back to Jaipur because I used to think, "How long I can keep working like this?" I started my career in the year 1985, and it had been good long 12 years since then. I had been travelling from city to city in my sales job, finally I decided to go back to my home town and start my business with my brother in Jaipur.

For the first 2 years, I tried to make things with my brother's business, but I was not meeting my ends. Then my father told me to expand and develop the business of Ayurvedic tooth powder which he used to sell on very small level, it was as small as earning Rs 3,000 per month only. Just imagine . . . ! How I could manage to survive with the meagre earnings of Rs 3,000 per month only, as compared to my previous earnings of Rs 30,000 per month.

I then joined my father's business as yet another opportunity and a task to grow it independently. I worked very hard day and night to develop the business of our 'Yunadent' ayurvedic tooth powder. Due to the lack of funds and production facility, I had no other options but to ask and appoint one of the local manufacturers as a Jobber (appointed manufacturer) to produce our Ayurvedic tooth powder for us under our brand name 'Yunadent' as per our formulation, quality and standards, as the formulation was developed by my father. That Jobber was not a person with a decent track record in his dealings. At that time I had no other options but to appoint him to do our Job work. I started getting our goods manufactured from him, and I used to pay him 75 paisa per unit of tooth powder bottle which he was manufacturing for us.

Up till year 2004, I had put in lot of efforts in creating this brand by advertising in various media, such as, newspapers, magazines, cinema halls, wall paintings, leaflet distribution, participating in several exhibitions, etc. During that period, my Jobber started feeling that he was not earning sufficient money and the margin of 75 paisa to Rs 1.25 per bottle was not an enough amount which he was getting. His mind was deviated to a wrong track. He decided to "Stab on my back" by applying for trademark of the product which I was promoting day and night with my hard work. He thought that if he gets the trade mark registered in his name, then he would stop manufacturing it for us. His intentions were to unethically snatch our brand and to capture the entire market share for becoming a millionaire. I was ignorant about his malicious intentions.

I was doing my routine business activities religiously. Although I had applied for getting the trade mark registered on my company's name, but my trade mark registration process was kept pending due to the ignorance of our local attorney at Jaipur.

It was on 3rd Jan 2006 early morning when one of my friends called me and asked me, "Did you see today's news paper? There is an advertisement which says that you are no more the owner of your brand 'Yunadent'. Your Jobber has grabbed it by doing some misrepresentation in the Court of trade mark authority."

When I saw that advertisement in newspaper, I was shocked for a moment and felt as if I had no ground under my feet. I immediately showed the newspaper to my wife and said, "Look at a declaration in the newspaper, finally this rascal has done the same as of what I feared."

It was the day of biggest "Crises" in my life, when suddenly I had lost my brand for which I had worked day and night, and spent millions of Rupees. I had only one brand to run my business. I immediately called my brother and one of my good friends to discuss with them, and asked for the best lawyer in town for consulting the way out to fight with this situation.

I then visited to the best lawyer in Jaipur, who is one of the eminent lawyers in India too. I told him the entire story. He then immediately passed his verdict as if he was a Judge in the Court of law that, "Mr Vohra, you have lost your brand and you cannot get it back now."

At such a distress situation, it was somewhat like having the biggest blank in my mind. I was thinking a series of questions about my uncertain future, such as:

1. Would I be left empty handed . . . ?
2. Would I have to restart my life once again?
3. Would I get into deep depression due to losing our brand, which I made with my hard work and experience of 14 years?
4. Would I be called a fool among the fraternity where I was considered to be very smart, intelligent, confident and successful person?
5. What image I would carry in my own eyes that one tiny litter thief has stolen my brand from my hands?
6. What answer I would give to the spiritual images of my mother and father (who died in year 1989 and 2000 respectively) to whom I worship every day?
7. What next could I do . . . ? Did I fall from the top of the hill?

It was exactly the situation that most suitably exemplifies as the "Crises" of one's life.

The lawyer charged Rs 7000 for the consultation of just 15 minutes. After coming back from the lawyer's office, I mentally reorganised myself and had a deep thought to the entire episodes of past 5 years. I concluded, "Truth cannot fail, and I will win because I am a truthful person. I never cheated anybody knowingly, so nothing can go wrong with me."

I further discussed with my brother and he suggested me the name of one of Mumbai based attorney of trademarks. I immediately called the attorney and told him the entire story over the phone itself (as I was not mentally prepared to go to Mumbai). I then got the answer from him about the fate of my brand. He replied me after listening carefully, "Rohit, I think you have a chance to win as per your story, but send me all the relevant papers. I will take up the matter to the Registrar of Trademarks for cancellation of trademark which was taken through misrepresentation by the other party." His statement was like the only Ray of Hope about the case, which came to my life at that time.

After that, lots of legal affairs took place, several Court hearings and police harassments happened. The huge debt burden also came to my shoulder, as a result. I finally won the case in the honorable Court of law on 5th June 2008, after facing the long hardships of two and half years.

I am thankful to my attorney, advocate and associates for their kind support which led me winning the case. I am always thankful to my family, brother and all the concerned for providing me their generous support, care, guidance and blessings at such a time of Crisis in my life, which helped me winning the case. **Above all, I am thankful to God for his blessings over me which finally caused me winning the case in the Court of law.**

13. Worship your God—If you avoid

Worship can be the next resort to find solace, if one fails or remain into Crisis in spite of following the above steps. Whatever the religion or spiritual philosophy you observe or follow, just collect yourself and visit to your place of worship, i.e. Temple, Gurdwara, Church or Mosque. Just sit there and observe people visiting there, and ask yourself, "Have everybody coming to this sacred place never failed in their lives?" Ask God as many questions you want. Ask how you could do it better, and chant the traditional prayer. Request the God to help you succeed in your work. Tell him that next time you would be more alert and better prepared. Promise him that you would do you task wholeheartedly. Also think that if you do not succeed, you would not be broken, rather you would change the task of your dream goal because it might not the only goal or the dream in the world you were working for.

The world is full of opportunities, but before leaving the current goal forever, one must put in all possible efforts into it.

As mentioned earlier in this book, our destiny has 51% of role to play in our success. If we accept this fact, then we will understand and accept everything in our life as a part of it. We cannot push and control destiny in our favor. We must accept that, destiny always favors us to get whatever we can have due to it.

It reminds me of a small incidence that, "Once when I was posted in Punjab in the year 1993, at that time it was one of the terrorist dominated areas in India, and terrorism was at peak over there during those days. I was working there as a Sales Manager. Everyday all the buses used to halt for the day at about 6 p.m. and thereafter no means of transportation was available. I was rushing to the bus stand to catch the last bus. In my heart, I was praying to God for helping me to catch the bus. It was the last bus that could take me to reach home, but I was late by 5 minutes as the last bus had left the depot. So I cursed my luck. Then I called home and conveyed that, "I will not be coming home tonight as I missed the bus, and I am staying back in this town itself." I went to a hotel and stayed there. On next day morning I came to know that, the bus which I could not catch was abducted by the terrorists, and all passengers were threatened before they looted the bus. Then I thanked God for saving me, whereas prior to that I was cursing my luck and destiny without knowing the good part of it. We must see to every end as a good end or rather suitable end. God really helps those who believe in him.

BEWARE! As a blind worshiper, we might get dependent on God. By doing so, we might understate the importance of karma or the action, and do not diligently put our best work in action. So, the importance of worship comes parallel or predominantly next to the stage when we do our best action in performing the task, and not without it.

The major concept of this "Blue Book" ends here because when we reach step by step to this point, then there is a high probability of attaining success and peace in life, and we can further leave everything to God.

As it is difficult for anyone to be so systematic and disciplined in the course of life, therefore beyond this stage, this book has various other interesting things to say . . . !

14. Realize without prejudice—If you have done a mistake

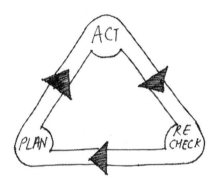

Plan—Act—Recheck—plan—Act—Recheck—plan . . .

In fact, the act of **realization** can be considered to be one of the creative and reformative acts of life. The expanse of realization may include any aspect of one's life. The following ideas may be served as the examples about the expanse of realization into one's own life:

1. The concept of **S**trengths, **W**eaknesses, **O**pportunities, **T**hreats (SWOT) analysis (as similar to managerial concepts) may be applied to realize the different aspects of one's own life.
2. Realize about one's potential, positive and negative traits.
3. Realize about one's desert attitude.
4. Realize about the fact that, one's own entity is just amongst one of the trillion factors of universe.
5. Realize about the necessity of understanding and adopting the truth, goodness, positive and fair attitude in life.

Once we realize such truths and facts, then we surely acquire a better position to deal with the junction. We should pray and express gratitude to God who may help us in realizing any situation.

Generally, people spend most of their time in judging others but not themselves. They do not evaluate or analyze themselves. They even cannot identify, "What went wrong . . . , or what was their own role in the root cause of problem?" It is like the most horrible thing in life.

The act of realization is meant for the goodness of all of us in order to plan and adopt the fair course of action for the future. So to find out about . . . what, why and how we might need to investigate into the cause and effect, we must analyze our own aspect. Let's then put our both good and bad part in front of ourselves and behave like a 'Judge'. When we act like a judge by putting both of our factors, then we not only understand the best part of our personality, but we can also help ourselves in a more judicious way to further develop our flawless personality. Therefore, the act of realization of facts and truths in life is must for everybody.

15. Repent without prejudice— One must do it.

We are not perfect human beings, and so we tend to make mistakes. If we do not make mistakes then it indicates that we do not try hard or try out new things. By not taking the inspirations or learning from the evident mistakes of others is not a sensible act. It is good to be careful for sensibly minimizing the mistakes and avoid making repeated or idiotic mistakes. It may not be considered as an insensible act to make normal mistakes in the process of learning, doing experiments, or getting new and enriching experiences, or trying to perform things in a different and better way. So there is no harm in making mistakes in order to learn or improve ourselves. On the other hand, repeating the same mistake carelessly may be an idiotic act, or it can be hypothetically compared to committing a crime which is a serious issue. Committing new mistakes may be fine but it is insensible to repeat the older mistakes, whether it harms anybody or not. Performing an act negligently and knowing that it would directly or indirectly harm others is a blunder, which is unforgivable. One must repent on such an act. As a matter of fact, repentance is a positive act because once we repent honestly it gives us an inner strength to proceed further. Repentance becomes a turning point for a person—be it a 'U' turn, 'L' turn, 'Y' turn or 'O' turn in life. All of these turns have got their own value. Repentance is a sort of appraisal, sooner it is done the better it is.

"It is better late than never," this proverb can be practically followed for the act of repentance to rectify any mistake in life. Do not repent with a new desire in mind, instead repent and act without desire.

Just think it over!

When I was in N.C.C. as a cadet, I used to go along with other cadets for camps in remote areas of the State. Once I was attending the Annual Training Camp (ATC) of N.C.C.—Air Wing, in year 1983 which was held near Kota, Rajasthan. We were sitting leisurely in late afternoon then suddenly a herd of sheep and lambs came along with their master from a nearby village. After the herd had crossed, one lamb was left behind and it entered one of our tents where we stayed. My friend went inside the tent, picked up a stick and hit the lamb with a notion to make him out of the camp area. Lamb tried to run but it was so badly hurt that it could not run and fell down near the tent itself. Then my friend went closer to lamb and further tried to push it with his leg, but the lamb could not even get up. My friend felt very sorry for having committed that sinful act. He picked up the lamb, brought it under a tree shade, made him drink water, and massaged the injured leg for a few minutes, but it was of no use. He was repenting on his deed.

He went to Commanding Officer of the camp, reported the incidence and asked for a solution so that he could take this lamb to a nearby veterinary hospital. He committed to himself that he would not eat anything till the time the lamb's injury gets healed and it starts walking. He then took this lamb to the veterinary hospital where the doctor examined the lamb and told my friend not to worry as the lamb had just a minor dislocation. Doctor then applied a gel ointment and bandaged the lamb, and said that by late evening the lamb would be fine. But it was not enough for my friend, and he took the lamb back in his arms and came back to the camp by local public transport. He did not have his dinner that night. On next morning when shepherd came to our campsite searching for his lamb, then my friend told him the entire story. By that time the lamb's leg had got repositioned and it could walk with a bit of limping movement.

Shepherd picked up the lamb and did not get angry at my friend's cruel act. Instead, he thanked him for treating it properly. My friend also gave him Rs 100 (which meant a lot of amount in the year 1983) for the treatment, and felt sorry for his act.

The episode was partially witnessed by me, but later on my same friend reported me the entire episode. It was like a learning experience which was performed out of sheer humanity. It was a true repenting act which was done without any expectation.

16. Rectify by heart—That is 'the way'

Generally a lot of opportunities for rectification of our mistakes come into our lives. Most of the times we do not understand the importance of rectification, or we really do not know about what or how to rectify because at that time we give priority to our rights than the duties, and so we try first to rectify others.

We tend to neglect the basic rules of ethics and just blindly convince ourselves that nothing went wrong, it was just an incidence which occurred by chance. Whereas, we should fairly evaluate the situation and should not try to convince ourselves with any biased thoughts! To become a good human being, we should first rectify ourselves.

Just think it over!

In the normal course of rectifying oneself, we can additionally evaluate the following factors that whether:

I could have done it in a bit better way:	Y/N
I was on the right direction:	Y/N
I was at the right place:	Y/N
I was at right time:	Y/N

I was with the right support system: Y/N
I was equipped with right kind of resources: Y/N
I was suitably responding to the situation: Y/N
I really gave a thought before applying last step: Y/N

After giving a thought to all these points or just answering them in 'Yes' or 'No', we may find ourselves in a better position to rectify and improve our lives.

Rectification does not mean that we have to compromise or change the course of lives. Rectification means to apply suitable and correct course of action at the given junction, which could not be done earlier. It is just about correcting the modus operandi which further helps us to proceed further towards our next junction.

17. Love has no substitute— Maintain your love

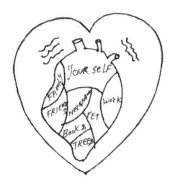

Love is the greatest power ever recognized by mankind.

It is very essential to keep the spirit of love alive, fresh and vibrant. I truly emphasize the need and importance of love, and everything in life seems futile or uninteresting without love. No matter what comes to life, which stage we are living in, how things are moving with us and we are moving in life. The best aspect of love is that we have to give it and forget. If it comes back to us then it triplicates our power. If it does not come back, it still doubles our power. By giving itself it gets double, whether it is received or recognized by others or not, whether it gives us the desired satisfaction or not. Person must love oneself or one's own life.

The expanse of love may include anything of the God's creation such as:

> To love and respect one's life partner, family, relationships and the support system. Love could be of romantic, platonic or spiritual nature.

> To love and work for the betterment of one's health, wealth, time, belongings, place and surroundings.

➤ To love one's work, inputs, zeal, goals, dreams, creations, point of view.

➤ To love and protect one's nation, culture, beliefs, ideologies.

➤ To love and foster peace and welfare of entire mankind, nature and environment.

➤ **Above all, love one's devotion to God.**

Love has the following qualities . . . :

☺ Love is peace
☺ Love is eternal
☺ Love is happiness
☺ Love is incomparable
☺ Love is not subjective
☺ Love is immeasurable
☺ Love is the power of growth
☺ Love is the motivational factor of life
☺ Love is an expression without expectation

Love itself means God.

18. Be Happy again—Happiness is the best fuel takes you up

It is a fact that happiness provides fuel to life, and it is the utmost thing for which the entire universal activities are being performed. If we do not get the happiness or satisfaction along with desired outcome, then we must question ourselves, "What we are living or working for . . . ?", "What will be there for us . . . ?" Even the achievement of our goals or success may seem worthless to us, if we do not get the happiness along with it at the end.

The feeling of happiness and satisfaction are interconnected with each other. The importance of happiness is equivalent to satisfaction to a certain extent, where happiness is satisfaction and satisfaction is happiness. It is explained in earlier topics that if we get satisfaction by our actions and circumstances, then it means that we are happy. On the other hand, we should not forget that being happy and satisfied does not mean to become stagnant or lag behind in our progressive life. Our dream goal might be still ahead, but happiness gives us the rejuvenation and courage to go further. It is a state of mind which varies from person to person. One who is not happy despite of getting abundance of fame, money or power; then his condition might actually be worse than that of a person having much lower status than him.

Different people may have their variety of different definitions about happiness which may or may not be superficial, materialistic, or related to their specific choices, interests or preferences. Apart from finding happiness in attaining the desired goals, or enjoying the things of liking and choices, or pursuing the hobbies, there may be innumerable reasons for a person to be happy.

A person may feel the happiness if:

- ✓ One speaks the truth.
- ✓ One has done his best.
- ✓ One believes in his deeds.
- ✓ One has paid his debt on time.
- ✓ One finds solution to any problem.
- ✓ One is accountable to himself only.
- ✓ One doesn't curse the circumstances.
- ✓ One sleeps on time and gets up early.
- ✓ One has accomplished his task on time.
- ✓ One follows the positive attitude towards life.
- ✓ One appreciates and promotes law and order.
- ✓ One doesn't compare his achievements with others.
- ✓ One can forgive, or behave modestly with people.
- ✓ One tries to follow the virtuous and right path in life.
- ✓ One desire less than he deserves (knows his own worth).
- ✓ One gets proper reward for his hard work or excellence.
- ✓ One thinks that he has not done any harm to others deliberately.
- ✓ One finds pleasure in doing any work with quality and excellence.
- ✓ One tries to follow a systematic, disciplined, healthy lifestyle, or tries to manage overall affairs of his life in a better way.
- ✓ One does any kind of social service or helps someone who needs him.
- ✓ One appreciates and protects the serene beauty of nature and the environment.
- ✓ One smiles at happy faces and tries to bring happiness to those who are sad.
- ✓ One appreciates or promotes the beauty of truth, faith, innocence and sanctity in human life.

Most important of all . . . , "One can become happy, if he wants to be happy!"

May God bless everyone to become happy! It may sound tough, but it is neither tough nor impossible to attain happiness as it is just a state of mind.

19. Desire instead of being greedy—
Evaluate the difference

Most of us cannot differentiate between desire and greed. Desire is permissible but greed is dangerous for us. How can we differentiate between them? In fact, the answer to this is really very simple. Desire is an act which has the base of our input capacity. On the other hand, greed is either out of our unethical input capacity or it is sheer joining the rat race. It can be seen around or it might be our own attitude that we sometimes wish to acquire or buy a thing which our friend or neighbor has bought. This attitude is called Rat race. Instead of heading towards an unknown end, when we desire something for us we must see its utility, worth and importance in our day-to-day life. Acquiring a luxury car may be a need for someone else, but it might be a sheer greed for ours if it is much beyond our affordability. Greed sometimes puts us on an unethical or illegal track for attaining the goal. If we honestly and sincerely work very hard to attain such higher goals as per our aspirations then it may not be called as greed.

A well known story "Fox and the grapes . . . ," can be recalled for describing greed. Once there was a fox in a jungle, she saw squirrels and birds eating grapes hanging on the branches of a grape plant. Fox never wanted the grapes actually, but when she saw others enjoy eating the grapes then greed pinched the fox, and she also wanted those grapes. Grapes were much above the ground level and out of her reach. Fox couldn't get the grapes after making several jumps, and finally she left the hope and said, "The grapes are sour."

It is definitely a very depressing attitude to blame the fruit, if it doesn't fall in our basket. No matter, we have the capacity to buy a thing or not, but we should definitely think that, "Do we really need it or not? Can it serve any long term benefit to us or not? Can it be maintained or sustained by us or not?" If we judiciously think upon these lines, and do not fulfill our greed through unfair means, then we may really lead a happy and peaceful life. Otherwise, attaining the object of our greed may drift us away from our self-respect and the path of humanity, which in turn is very dangerous. One should not make himself a short term friend and a long term enemy of oneself.

So, just be careful about it!

20. Never lose the self-esteem—Stick to your fundamentals

Let's once again focus over the importance of **self-respect**. If a person doesn't get the desired results on the right track even after having performed all the previous steps, then such a situation may lead a person to lose his self-esteem. There might be several factors coming to life due to which we may put our self-esteem at the second priority. We then manage to show it to others except in our own eyes. We should not degrade ourselves in our own eyes, and should never compromise with our self-esteem. Instead, we must reconsider all the facts, rework on our self-esteem and reorganize ourselves to work in the right direction. We should put our esteem in our own eyes first, then in the eyes of our parents, and loved ones, and so on . . . . Each and every detail about understanding the importance of maintaining the self-esteem is not needed to be clarified much at this step. We have to work towards it individually.

There is a great difference between 'self-esteem' and 'self-greed or self-ego'.

Just think it over!

21. Struggling is a part of the game—Keep pouring in . . .

L ife is full of struggle. There could be struggle for survival or to earn, achieve and maintain name, fame, wealth, progress and success in life. The struggle is unavoidable.

One may face the struggle at any time or place, in private or public life, in any form due to any of various reasons, situations and circumstances, or the other adversities of life, which may or may not be directly or indirectly within one's control such as:

- Negligence, indiscipline, mismanagement or immoral attitude in life
- Unhealthy competition
- Illegal practices
- Weak and improperly implemented legal system
- Weak or corrupt administrative and political system
- Various social problems
- Religious intolerance
- Improper observance of rights and duties by the people

- The struggle between fair and unfair, orthodox and modern, good and bad, virtuous and immoral, law and crime, illiberal and liberal philosophies
- The struggle arising due to different extremist, fanatic or radical ideologies which remain uncompromising and unfriendly with others.

All the ill deeds, selfish and unfair acts, practices or attitude of the people not only degrade themselves and raise problems, difficulties, troubles for themselves in the long run, but they also do a big harm to others and raise undue and unnecessary struggle in the life of others.

People sometimes unknowingly or negligently make themselves as the cause of raising innumerable instances of struggle into their own lives or into the lives of others. People can try to avoid raising any of various such struggles by leading a correct path of life. It can be easily understood about such unnecessary struggle with the 2 simple examples as under:

1. Suppose a person is very negligent about his own health and fitness over the long time, then he can definitely become weak or prone to illness, suffer medical problems and bad health, have reduced immunity, vitality, stamina and power, early aging, etc. It may definitely cause reduction in quality and quantity of its own life. **By doing so, he might definitely raise the struggle in his own life to regain his own health later on.** Any illness due to such negligent mistakes (which could be easily avoided by him) may also put his family members or caretakers into the unnecessary struggle of facing hassles. It also causes the overall wastage of time, money and financial crisis to his family.
2. Suppose if a person hits another person in a road accident due to his own negligence or disobeying traffic rules, then in such a situation he not only puts his own life in danger but he can also cause an injury and loss to the others involved, and raise an unnecessary struggle into the lives of both.

We can try to alleviate or rectify the causes of struggle to some extent which are within our own control, in an attempt to be a good human being, and to make a better life for ourselves and others. It can be easily done by us as under:

✓ By doing self-evaluation and rectifying our own mistakes (if any)

✓ By becoming very careful about life
✓ By managing our lives better
✓ By holding a positive, humane, open-minded, scientific, decently liberal and humane approach towards life
✓ By leading a disciplined, ethical and virtuous life
✓ By helping others
✓ By obeying and promoting law and order, etc.

Just imagine yourself to be in a large room filled with bubbles, as mentioned about bubbles in earlier topic of this book.

I am sure you may have a question in mind, "Why author named it bubbles?" So let's discuss about it. The various positive or negative activities, situations, phases or struggles in our lives which may affect the course of our lives, may be conceptually compared to bubbles.

Have you noticed the lifespan of any bubble . . . ?

I am sure you know that each bubble is nothing but a delicate blown water-shield which is short-lived. It survives until it is hit by a 'slightly stronger air breeze' or by a 'bit harder surface than its own'. It may burst even by a minor change in 'ambient temperature'. This phenomenon applies to all the bubbles. Try to apply such a similar change in condition phenomenon (as that of a bubble) into present situation of your life, and you may witness the change in condition or direction of your life.

Concept of bubbles can thus be applied to human life. Any of the changeable, controllable or short-lived situations and moments that acts as a temporary or decisive phase in person's life, can be conceptually compared to that of a bubble. It has potential to directly or indirectly affect the course of one's life. Life is full of such bubbles, and they are much weaker than our thoughts. Nothing is long-lived.

Following are the phases, situations, moments, feelings, incidences or circumstances which are like bubbles:

➢ Money, success or fame.
➢ Moments of excitement, enjoyment, smile, hug, handshake or kiss.

- ➤ Moments of anger, tension, depression, guilt, hatred, boredom, mistake, hurdle or failure.
- ➤ All the turning points in our lives.
- ➤ All the previous inputs in our lives.
- ➤ Moments of meeting or departing from others.
- ➤ Day and night are like bubbles.
- ➤ Life itself is like a bubble due to its uncertain and unpredictable nature.

Yes! What is not a "Bubble" is the Almighty God.

One must understand the fact that nothing is permanent in this universe. If there is anything which is permanent, is the change. **"Only the change is permanent."** The process of change continuously takes place in and around our life, and in the world or universe. No one can stop the change. The almighty power is "One".

Let's believe that:

1. Our **positive** efforts and actions will always help us in life. It might not show any immediate, expected or tangible results, but surely it gets deposited into life's bank account and comes back at the right time on right maturity date, that too with an interest. The best part of life is that one never knows about the maturity time of any hard work done by him. And also, one never knows about where or in which form the results would come.
2. On the other hand, our **negative** actions might give us temporary or undue advantage, but it also gets deposited into life's bank account, and it will definitely degrade or harm us (with interest) in the long run, at any time, place or in any form.

22. Patience—It is a virtue

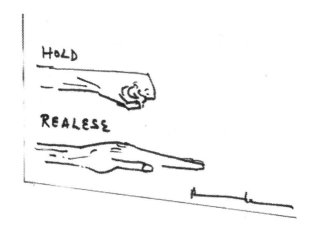

Patience is the next parallel factor in the entire course of life. It has been observed that patience grow with the age such as:

At the age of 4 months—Patience is absolutely absent.

At the age of 4 years—It hardly exists.

At the age of 14 years—It is very less.

At the age of 24 years—It gets increased.

At the age of 42 years—It is far better.

At the age of 62 years—It is tremendous.

And so on . . . .

Why does is happen?

As a matter of fact, our patience grows as we grow in our life—"Mentally".

It is very difficult to keep your patience when situation does not allow your mind to do so. When situation is such that, you cannot stop yourself without reacting, then it is the time for you to check your patience, which means that you should act or react in such a way that it should not add fuel to the fire.

Your action or reaction should be a "neutralizer-cum-favorable" work. At the end of Game . . . , you will win over the situation, if you keep this in mind in any situation.

Let me ask you a Question, "What will you do if you see your father in his extreme anger, when you know that he is wrong?"

Just apply the simple formula of "Neutralizing-cum-favoring" step.

You can say, "My dear Dad, I do agree with you . . . , and if I were at you place then I would have been exactly the same what you are as of now." (Then after giving 45 seconds break, you can say, "But Dad . . . as a matter of fact I think . . . *"Say, what you know as the fact . . . ."*)

Such a method will always help you to develop your patience.

Other example:

"Suppose you know that somebody has harmed you or regularly harming you, then how you can keep your patience intact."

Answer is again simple:

Instead of reacting or saying anything else . . . , you just say, "Well I think, I am not capable to work/live/play xyz with you . . . . Can we sit and close the matter forever?" This expression of yours will give a big 'Jerk' to him, and you will find a lot of space for correction, and even if it is not corrected then you are already prepared to close it forever.

So take care of yourself.

If you are angry and already lost your patience then recall this method, "Just say to yourself—Relax, relax, relax . . . ."

Then say to yourself, "Tomorrow will be the finest day, and things will become better—Relax, relax and just relax. Blow three deep breathes and drink 3 full glasses of water."

Hope you will remember that "Patience is a virtue"!

23. Differentiate between Smart and Hard work—Easy to understand

(like you just noticed a right tilt in above sketches,
you still have to search the differences)

Working hard and working smart are the two different ways to do the work. We cannot ignore one of them. One has to be a hard worker, but at the same time the hard work should be done smartly. The smartness means having, using or showing the quick witted intelligence.

The smart work is done by understanding the given situation as quick as possible, and by putting the most suitable inputs actively and optimally into the work, for example, suppose you are a medical sales representative (MR), and if you get a chance then you may wish to meet many doctors within 3 hours at outpatients' department (OPD) in the hospital. There you may find lot of patients waiting for their turn to consult the doctor. It is the doctor's duty and priority to examine his patients first. So as a MR, you may have to wait for a long time to get a chance to promote your product. If you wait there for 2-3 hours to get your chance, then such a waiting may not be called a hard work. **In such a situation, it depends**

on you as a MR that how you smartly act and manage your overall time and work over there. It may reflect your smartness if:

✓ You send your visiting card inside the doctor's chamber with an interesting note overleaf, or give an infectious smile and warm body gestures when you get a chance to see a doctor.

✓ You mentally organize yourself to be ready for giving your effective presentation, or to plan your other important work.

✓ You give an impactful, dynamic and impressive presentation about your product within a short span of 60-90 seconds, as and when you get a chance to meet a doctor in his chamber.

24. Focus on the task—If you tend to lose focus

(Arjuna and Dronacharya episode of aiming for bird's eye clearly mentioned in Maha bharat)

We must focus or concentrate upon one thing at a time. Most of the people think that they can work on more than two things simultaneously, but they are highly mistaken. We might consider to do more than one thing at a time but it is a fact that we are incapable of doing both of the works with equally high quality and excellence, and so we should avoid to do dual acts. When we are on the track towards our goal, we must see only the goal.

Let's understand it in a better way as under:

While working towards the target, we should consider only one single specific target in front of us. We must consider our target 'as big as elephant' in front of us, no matter how tiny or far the target is from us.

The word elephant is used here to lay emphasis upon the target. If the target is deviated from our focus, we tend to postpone the result or we might fail. Just recall about Arjuna in the epic of Mahabharata. Guru Dronacharya once asked the five Pandavas one by one to hit the eye of a bird sitting on a tree, while giving bows and arrows in their hands, and further asked about what they saw in front of them?

One of Pandava replied, "He could see the sky, tree and bird over there." Two of them said, "They could see the tree and brown bird sitting on branch of the tree." Another one said, "He could see a bird moving its head left and right." Whereas Arjuna replied, "Guru ji, I can clearly see at an 'eye target of the bird', where you asked me to hit the arrow."

We can see that a minor difference in their focus could easily drift them from the target. It was Arjuna only who could hit exactly at the bird's eye in the first go. It is the basic law of life which determines that how accurately we can produce the results in shortest possible time, and it is possible only when we are focused.

Believe me! We may enjoy a lot while doing our work when are focused. Being focused gives immense pleasure and the work can be done comfortably.

25. Regaining confidence—If you have lost it

(Recall Lord Hanuman's episode, 'the time just before—when he was asked to go Lanka for the first time.' even he re gained it than—clearly mentioned in Ramayan)

It is necessary to put reemphasis over the topic of **confidence** at this stage, as already mentioned earlier. It is because we all are human beings and we don't follow or understand even the easiest or important things by just hearing or reading it once.

After reviewing this topic, the importance and meaning of confidence may not be forgotten by the valued readers. I feel pleasure in putting reemphasis on the power of confidence. So, it is just as a reminder!

It is very important for us to really understand the hairline difference between the confidence and overconfidence.

Confidence is our best friend, whereas overconfidence is our worst enemy. It generally becomes difficult for anybody to understand the difference between two of them. Such difference can be easily understood in a simpler way as under:

> ➤ It is the **confidence** when we believe in our capability while managing or dealing with any situation coolly and comfortably.
> ➤ It is the **overconfidence** when we feel excited and proud of our inner power to win. As a matter of fact, winning might not be anything too big for us but when we hold a careless attitude and deal a situation with an assumption of winning, then such a careless attitude or act may indicate our overconfidence.

We may sensibly become a better confident if we realize or follow the tips as under:

> ✓ We should remain cool, calm and careful while dealing with any situation in life.
> ✓ We should express our certainty about success, only after achieving the same.
> ✓ We should neither overestimate our own capabilities, nor underestimate the target.
> ✓ It is good to be happy with our capabilities, knowledge or experience to maintain our confidence level, but we should try to carefully examine the complete situation and should act accordingly with best of our efforts.

26. Habit of winning—keep improvising your skills

We must strategically plan our line of action by carefully using our full knowledge, experience and common sense, and also by collecting more and more references from the past. We should further try to reaffirm the collected references with the success stories of others. On the other hand, we must remain very careful about not to copy someone else's plan, as it may be dangerous because other person might have his own circumstance and resources to deal with his situation, which may differ from us. Once we plan our own line of action, then we must check it and act upon it. When we start following our line of action, then we must keep rechecking and redirecting it frequently for getting adapted to any changes in circumstances during the course of action. This triangle will help you to proceed further and it the most secure manner.

Fundamentally it is always better to have the 2 contingency plans at a time in addition to 1 prime plan of action in which we have done our home work well. If we do so, then it is sure that our chances of failure would reduce to minimum.

Let's proceed further. It is the time to 'Act' upon the line of action at this stage. Act with full confidence, truthfulness and positive attitude. While acting, it should be remembered not to take undue advantage of other's weakness, but one should try to win fairly with his own strengths. It must be emphasized upon the words "Just Do It" at this stage, and do it with an approach that one is giving his best and nothing less than the best. One would not wait for the results to follow in his favor.

Many a times, if the result not follows in one's favor, then it might be a kind of an indirect favor for him. One should never lose hope, patience and positive attitude in life. If a person has given his best, then it is sure that the best sustainable, prudent and virtuous power would definitely come into him sooner or later. If result comes early in one's favor as expected, then he must keep up his confidence and working spirit as before. If the result does not come as per one's expectations, then he should replan it further to start working on it again with the same enthusiasm and confidence as earlier. It is a bit difficult but not impossible. Later on, one would realize that the delay had taught him various lessons and given rich experiences to become more careful and patient, which may further help him in achieving dream goal.

Once a person wins, he feels like being on top of the World—"His own 'personal' World." He feels happy, confident, thrilled, proud, powerful and satisfied, and likes to celebrate the occasion. He shares all of these feelings with everyone, and receives appreciation and congratulations in return. He starts liking every damn thing on the earth at that occasion, and spends to collects various things. He feels himself to be the master of that specific junction. He might become a bit careless and start talking big, or start giving guidelines to others. He might be called by authorities who recognize his work. It is really a great moment when a person wins his dream goal or a part of his dream goal. The victory reminds of an old saying, "All is well that ends well."

It is the time to check one's emotional life. One should try to bring professionalism and modesty in his achievements. One should control himself and remain "down to earth". He should welcome the appreciation with grace and humbleness while being thankful to the contribution of people involved (if any) in one's success. Above all, one should be thankful to God for his blessings into one's success. It is the time for a person to start working on his next dream plan, instead of getting driven away with the recent success.

"Achieving the next goal in sequence of dream goal must be one's aim," in an attempt to constantly survive and to keep up with the pace of life.

Life is full of uncertainties and unforeseen circumstances which may cause frequent ups and downs in the course of anyone's life. Such circumstances acts like ascending or descending escalators in life. (It is like two escalators moving side by side, first one of which goes up, and the second one comes down.) It may be okay if a person takes rest for sometimes after having won a particular goal, but such a rest should not be prolonged for long because in such a case, the descending escalator No.2 (as mentioned) may get initiated to bring him down in life. Therefore one should get up and proceed towards the next goal for attaining new heights, even faster than the speed of such descending escalator of life.

Be careful that we practically do not find any such No.1 sort of ascending escalator in life, where we can comfortably stand upon. On the other hand, it is actually our own everlasting spirit of pursuing newer or higher goals, efforts to achieve them and maintaining the sequence of success acts as the ascending escalator in life.

27. Lay down milestones—If you feel stagnated

MILE STONES

(no matter what your age / gender / proffesion is)

Repeat the success: It is more important to remain a winner than to be 'No.1 for just once'. After having won once, it becomes the need of a person to repeat success for the reasons that one has to achieve dream goal ahead, and it is also expected of him to be a winner by the others because now others put more faith in him 'than he might have in himself'. One has to keep his faith alive in oneself. It is a fact that, once a person experiences and enjoys the success then he likes to maintain it further. If he do not honor and maintain success, then he may face adverse comments from others for doing so. People might interpret . . . , "Well, it was just by chance that he got the success, and actually he was not capable of it."

If a person doesn't maintain the success then even he may also subconsciously doubt of his own capabilities, so it basically becomes one's own urge to keep winning again and again. It is not just one's own choice to remain a winner but it is also the price that he has to pay for his future. In other words, one has to follow all previous acts genuinely with the same attitude that he kept earlier, and the rest of everything may then be left to God.

The universal law applies that, "Give your best, and best will come back to you." Let's understand that success is not in one's hands but the inputs are within our control. Success is like a milestone and not like an end of the journey. One should keep adding successes into life because it maintains power and dominance into its respective field.

The number of success milestones that we lay in life helps us to become a leader or veteran later on. Our personality then becomes our yardstick for other, and we can help others to get benefit from our knowledge and experience.

'Success milestones' are the pillars which always stand along with our personality to make us feel tall or grand.

28. Build your Fort—If you want to secure your goodwill forever.

Fort of growth and success: When a person sets good number of success milestones in his life, then there onwards it comes the time for him to make his "fort of growth". It means to create one's position in the society for other to look upon, or getting it endorsed by eminent personality, or highlighting and expanding one's worth by coming into the limelight of society, be it then social work, sponsorships, society building activities, besides doing your different business. By doing so, a person acquires the status of a leader in his field. Then people tend to swear by his name, or they treat him as their idol. In other words, a person then attains the status of being a master in his own field, no matter whether he is a student, businessman, professional, serviceman or a social worker.

Person should enjoy such a position with modesty and grace, and retain it with great regards towards others while maintaining his own dignity and importance. He should generously share his thoughts while valuing others, encourage the beginners and guide others to reduce the common mistakes and shortcomings which could cause failure in life. He should quote his struggling moments without boasting upon his own strengths. He should not become a proud or self-praising person.

He should decrease the distance from people when people comes closer to him, and his personality would become larger than life or become a living legend.

29. Shine as a star and spread like air—

After attaining previous stage, it then comes the time for a person to expand or spread his wings easily as wide as possible, especially without any exertion. If the wings are spread with exertion then it means that his fort still needs more reinforcements with successful events. In other words, before doing the expansion, his worth, power or dominance should be made as strong as a fort, so that no one (whether it is his own support system, time, competitors, or his own ignorant attitude) could damage it.

When a person has enjoyed the supremacy and protection of his success, then it is quite possible that he tends to take the "functions" for granted. Just be careful not to take anything for granted, not even "yourself"!

Once a person has spread comfortably, then success follows him naturally and he could get the winning stride. It gives you a very long-term security and the comforts of coming decades. One should be careful that such security and comforts are not forever, they would also definitely change because it's only the change which is permanent.

Even after achieving such a stage, one should keep oneself active and lively to explore other avenues in life. To move further, one should make new dreams and follow all the steps as mentioned in previous topics of this book.

30. Renounce it (The semi-final word)— You need to leave for next generation

Renounce: After having achieved enough for this life, he must think of renouncing it. He has to do it on one fine day, if he wishes to live forever by his name. It can be witnessed that several successful sportsperson renounce their game by deciding not to play it any more. The similar step is taken by various eminent people, great politicians, businessmen, etc. To seek the spiritual peace, several Hindus renounce their family and social lives, and goes to pilgrimages and holy shrines for rest of their lives, after having successfully lived their worldly lives.

One should renounce for the betterment of his own and the welfare of society. Above all, one should renounce for the sake of gaining spiritual enlightenment or to attain God. Renouncing is a very satisfying act, and it can be easily experienced or observed as per the spiritual philosophies that, **"One can get the higher level of satisfaction in leaving or giving something, as compared to the satisfaction derived in taking or acquiring the same."** Renouncing means a person gives up his desires or expectations about any relation, person, place, thing or materialistic attractions, 'except God'. At such a stage, a person lives with only one desire left with him and it is to be 'with God'. He then becomes like a baby who wishes to sleep in the lap of his mother or father (here, mother or father refers to 'God'). He wants to gain and enjoy the spiritual security, serene peace and happiness under the supreme almighty power because he has a desire to leave his body behind and to eagerly dissolve in the almighty **God** soul called *Parampita Parmeshwar.*

31. Get dissolved (It is the final word)—
You need to get Bliss

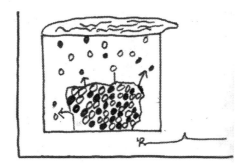

Dissolve: Get dissolved like ice in the water, as if you came from the water and became an ice like creature which had to vanish one day.

A person is born without his own choice, his body is given by his parents and his soul is gifted by God. A kid who do his homework and class work sincerely, feels himself eligible to get the special care, appreciation or reward from his parents. Similarly, a person also feels to act like such a kid in front of God at the stage of renouncement, after having done his best (as in this book) and has no regrets for whatever he delivered or performed. He then feels to forward a request and prays to God that, "May I sleep or get Moksha forever . . . ," as I would only be relaxed by doing so.

At this stage, one should pray as much as possible. Almighty God might hear a person and allow him to get dissolved into it. God could also say through his divine or spiritual inspiration that, "You are a true representative of humankind, and I want you to stay there just go beyond to serve, lead and preach the humankind. I will call you back on the day it is written in your destiny."

After all, destiny is destiny and not a destination where we can reach by choice or demand.

It is great! Once God directs a person to stay back, it is again a wonderful moment, because one obeys his inner voice—"the voice of God" as directed to him in a supernatural way. He would again perform, and this time not for oneself but to serve the humankind.

On this stage, the brief description about a 'Jeev' finishes here. Beyond this Junction, it is the stage of *Anuyayi* (the follower) that continues . . . .

End of SECTION—3

SECTION 4

Stage / Junction No.2
Anuyayi
(The follower)

A person can be called to be a *"Anuyayi"* (the follower) of Almighty God, if he believes and practices that:

a) Somebody is bigger and brighter than him in this world.
b) He speaks only truth.
c) The acts and deeds delivered by him in present will not be a cause of regret in future.
d) Everything in the universe is directly or indirectly associated with him, and he has no right to destroy or degrade it, as he is not a Generator.
e) He is just as a tiny particle. He can give support to the world (as per one's capability) and doesn't expect anything in return because the suitable and desiring result will take its own course for coming back to him in life.

f) He is happy for being alive.

g) He gets various opportunities by the grace of God, and after utilizing them he will leave them one day with the feeling of no regrets or fear.

h) He is nothing without the support of others, relations, things, knowledge. And he is surviving in the world just because of them.

i) He is not the sole master of his own body, but it was given to him by his parents, and it is his lifetime duty to respect and take care of his parents.

j) His 'soul' is given to him by God, and can be taken back from him without any prior notice.

k) He has to take care of God's creation in any form.

When a person assimilates the above set of philosophy in oneself then he is called as *Anuyayi* (follower), the passenger of spiritual journey.

There are millions of people in the world. Each individual is different from another. Every individual may have his own specific opinion about the preachers and Gurus who deliver their thoughts, guidelines and mode of life in various ways.

In the course of self-developed knowledge, several myths also get developed. Such myths may lead to different findings. If one structures his course of life upon self-developed knowledge and myths, then he cannot attain Moksha (Bliss).

One who repents of his wrong actions with total truthfulness and corrects himself, he then restarts with full confidence and new zeal as per religious beliefs is called *Sathyarthi* (truth believer).

This time work should be done keeping the state of mind that, "Whatever will be the outcome, it would be acceptable to me and I deserve only that, nothing other than that, whether it is in my favor or not."

One should observe that he would become more and more knowledgeable as he learns. He would also realize about the limited level of his own knowledge just by gaining the same.

The expanse of knowledge is limitless in fact. So it would be absolutely wrong if a person believes that he has achieved the *Gyan* (knowledge).

Whereas, considering oneself to be on the track of acquiring knowledge or practicing earned knowledge would be more appropriate.

If we just look around and ask ourselves a question that, "Are we associated directly or indirectly with the place, things, living beings, power and the change occurring around us . . . ?" Then, some of us might answer it 'Yes', other may answer it 'No', and some may say 'We do not know.'

Suppose a person gives an affirmative answer to the above question, then he may be considered to be a knowledgeable person to a great extent, for holding such an ideology that, "We all are the tiny little parts of Great Universal Laboratory, the basic purpose of which is Humanity, and that is why we are all associated with each other through Humanity."

If a person holds an idea about or visited or worked at Physics, Chemistry or Biology laboratories, such as in school; then he might have observed that such labs are very specific to their subjects. The teachers give various guidelines to students for operating the lab. The student obeys all the given guidelines without any hesitation because he knows in the core of his heart that, "My teacher is right and I must follow him."

We humans are also like such students, and a part of the universe. We are dependent on someone, and attached with the rules, and associated with a team. Above all, we are not the only one for whom this lab is existing, this great lab is called universe. The single law for all of us is Humanity, which has got various subtitles to understand and to be explored. We will discuss them in the coming topics.

Our life style depends upon various factors, such as, our attitude, nature, mindset, personality, working capacity, background, heritage and above all on stars and planets up there in the sky.

When a creature comes into existence, it is born at a particular place and time. Earth rotates at a fixed pace and revolves around the Sun. The moon, planets or celestial bodies also keeps on moving, and each one of them is at some specific astronomical location in the sky at every point of time. Each celestial object releases various types of rays which reaches on earth directly or indirectly, and envelops each and every part of earth. When a 'person' is born at a particular place and time, then variety of rays from different celestial bodies falls at particular angle over that person according to their respective astronomical positions. The rays which enter into person's body at the time of his birth determine his 'course of life'. That is how he acts in life, or carry on his health. The location of celestial bodies in the sky at the time and place of person's birth becomes his ruling Sun sign and that determines his life. All such astrological activities at the time of person's birth indicate his destiny too. Such an astrological phenomenon can be understood by reading "Indian *Panchaang*" or some of the birth sign books available in western countries known as Horoscopes.

So let's go beyond and understand the same. Just like the above, every creature has its own destiny. Every creature is associated with each other.

Do you know that, there might be an indirect or long chain of relation between tiger (in jungle) and the electricity (in home)?

Let's understand that, tiger lives in a jungle and we live in urban area. We use the electricity in our homes for using various electrical or electronic appliances, which eases our lives. Perhaps it may seem that there is no relation between a tiger and the electricity, but by using a word 'perhaps', we create an investigation possibility for the readers to find out the relationship between them.

Tiger lives in a jungle, and if tiger is not there then the population of wild herbivorous animals would keep on increasing which would further eat up the entire vegetation of jungle. When they would not have anything to eat, then they would also die of starvation. Therefore, a chain of such interrelated activities would slowly and gradually diminish the existence of entire jungle along with its entire flora and fauna. Once jungle is turned into desert, then there would be no rains because jungle and greenery attracts the clouds of rain, and it puts a very dynamic effect on climate of the vast expanse of area. If it doesn't rain, then it can cause drought and famine. The streams and tributaries do not flow to supply the water of rivers, and underground water level also decreases. Then water levels of rivers decreases and they gradually become dry.

When rivers become dry, then dams built across them also gets dry which in turn cannot generate hydroelectric power. So the hydroelectric power produced from such a natural source also ceases, and is not made available to people for use.

Isn't it amazing that we can find an indirect and long chain of interrelation between the tiger and hydroelectric power (which can even be used to play the music system)! Therefore we can easily observe or investigate thousands of such interrelations between various different things around us. Whenever we identify them, we understand their importance, and keep on realizing the universal law of interdependence. In the same way, we may understand the value of all human beings and creatures, and we may grow up as knowledgeable human beings.

Let's go beyond this point to discover few more facts about us.

The sequence and coordination of uncertain happenings in life can be understood by the knowledge of *Braham*. In this context, the 'uncertain happenings' indicates the outcome of the actions of *Agyani* (a person in worldly darkness) because he does not know what is going to be next, while 'sequence and coordination' is used here for a *Gyani* (brilliant person) because he is aware of the fact that every happening has its history and reason to have happened.

To easily understand it further, let's look at an example. A businessman that does his business activities today puts an effect on its profits and growth in short time or coming months, whereas, a man earning on daily wage basis barely manages his immediate needs and feeds his family for a day or two. On the other hand, the God almighty continuously keeps on weaving his billions of acts just within a fraction of second, which determines or decides the course of the future of human beings on the basis of their deeds, which is called as the destiny of human beings. God keeps all such future acts waiting to be happened in the womb of time, and every next second, he keeps on implanting and executing new destiny on the basis of the deeds of human beings. The limited vision of human beings can estimate the probability but not the facts behind their destiny. At the same time, God gives us an opportunity to understand the circumstances so that the best course of action can be performed by us accordingly on the present situations.

By our Karma (work input) we make our future, and by our intentions we make our 'luck'. Just like the cloth keeps getting weaved. With our karma and intentions we can achieve the fruits (results). Author has written fruit as the result because whatever it may be, it should be taken and should be received as 'fruit'. Fruit means, freshness along with energy. The energy gives comfort, which further causes happiness. The happiness can be understood as a means of peace. And finally the peace is considered to be equivalent to a sort of Moksha (the Bliss).

Expecting the fruit is not bad or wrong but expecting the desired fruit is inappropriate, and working towards the goal by keeping the desired fruit in mind may be considered as unacceptable in spiritual sense. It is just like a person who is walking ahead but in reverse motion, and watching the travelled track with a fear that he might get lost. Whereas, a *Sadhak* (professional) keeps walking with his vision while making his way from jungle to mini-walkway, to a lane, to a street and then to a highway of life.

The person who walks with his vision has no regrets and he believes in a saying, "Let bygones be bygones." He keeps walking with a faith that he is a truthful person, and is getting matured and developed day by day. Development itself is an upliftment, and upliftment is the fruit in itself. If he gets desired or anticipated fruit, then he should take it as a bonus.

If somebody tries and succeeds in getting the fruits by any unfair means, then he may just get its temporary and short-term benefit only without any fulfillment because such an act is never blessed by God, and it also puts a multifold negative impact on one's destiny in any form anytime in future. We deserve only such a fruit which is ripened by our acts of full devotion, focal concentration, hard work, while retaining our self-respect.

If we wish to give any sort of security and safety to ourselves, then we may put ourselves under someone to avail his protection, or have a feeling that someone is above us, and he is the God Almighty. Let's go to almighty's *Sharan* (protection) and leave ourselves in his coupe. Once we do it, we may enjoy his security and safety to the utmost satisfaction because nothing is bigger and better than God.

It is a saying that, "To err is human . . ." and it is natural for all of us to commit mistakes. On the other hand, to wear an attitude of negligence or making mistakes repeatedly (not rectifying the same), and not giving up the bad habits and erroneous path in life which leads a person to commit mistakes, can be considered to be as bad as a crime.

In an attempt to nullify one's own mistakes, **a person should think before he speaks or acts**. It is sure that half of the problems in one's life may cease to arise, if a person carefully self-evaluates his each course of thought and action beforehand. By doing so, he may repent at his erratic course of action (if he finds) at thought level, and rectify the same to nullify the probability of making mistakes before they actually occur. It is incumbent that one's intentions should be generously honest, genuine and unbiased towards the process of repentance. One should be 100% sure to have zeroed his own mistake level, and then start in its direction with an attitude that, whatever is going to come back to me is actually what I deserve.

As mentioned earlier, thinking oneself to be suitable for getting desired result is inappropriate. It may mislead us towards greed, and greed may lead us towards anger. Instead of this, accepting the fruit as it comes to us, gives us peace and happiness. If we have done our best, then such uncertainty about fruit is due to our own destiny as determined by God. Life is a sequence and coordination of uncertain happenings, and acknowledging the same can be taken as the knowledge about destiny in particular sense.

As a matter of fact, most of the part and partial of a human being does not belong to him in a real sense. Yes! We must acknowledge such a hard fact. Let's understand it in a simple way. The body of a person is given to him by his parents, and his soul is given by the God Almighty. Did a person make it himself? The answer is a simple 'No'. Then another factor is about mind which acts as a driver of his life, and it is again ruled by the circumstances. Can he rule the circumstances fully? Can he really change his surroundings, or direct the course of his life fully as per his own choices? Again the answer to such questions is 'No' to a large extent. On the other hand, the materialistic possessions earned or possessed by him can also be lost anytime due to any reason which is beyond one's control, such as, theft, robbery, fraud, fire, natural calamities, etc. So, what else belongs to him in a true sense? Therefore, saying that nothing belongs to a person seems to be true to large extent. It is exactly in support of an ideology as mentioned in earlier pages that, "We all are tiny little parts of Great Universal Laboratory, the basic purpose of which is Humanity . . . ," Then, why most of us forget the rule of not obeying the universal law?

Why do we become our own teachers and start making our own laws, instead of following this Great Universal Laboratory? Why don't we follow the restrictions and guidelines as laid down by our supernatural legal system? And, why do we keep damaging the established laws of nature and keep ourselves busy in making the new way of life one without knowing its repercussion?

Development is not a bad idea, but development by destroying the proven past is pathetic. (Please refer to 'Vedas' for all such proven methods of life.)

In this human world, our everyday destiny (God's decided destination) gives us a new question paper and new problems to solve. God notices how successfully we solve them with the help of all our six senses. The **five** senses commonly relates to our eyes, nose, ears, skin, tongue, and the **sixth** sense is our mind at its conscious and subconscious level, which can utilize our perception, knowledge and experience at optimum level. Besides, mind is also the master of all other five senses, and it can be disciplined, directed, trained or conditioned towards achieving excellence in life, or for the spiritual upliftment and enlightenment of oneself, or to become a good human being. If we pass in such an examination, then we get upgraded which we can be observed by ourselves in our day to day life, and we can thereby called a student of knowledge.

If we fail in such an examination then we need to rework on them.

If we live a happy life, then it means that we are upgrading ourselves, but whenever we divert our focus from the subject, we tend to degrade or fail then.

This proposition of our life is accounted by God and he fills our future log book with various happenings. Whenever we reach to the future date (as a matter of fact, 'today' as the future date of our history), we face a particular set of circumstances as per our destiny which is decided by God as a result of our past events. Sometimes it may be favorable and sometimes not. When circumstances are favorable we enjoy them but when circumstances are adverse we curse them, and try to by pass them as if they are not ours, and tend to oppose them. We tend to find faults in others, and often ask to ourselves that, "Why it happened with me, I didn't do anything wrong." As a matter of fact, our subconscious mind questions us, "What was that I did wrong?" If we realize its cause, then we must correct it, and then proceed further.

It is always a good time for a person to learn from his past mistakes. He should immediately rectify the cause of problem, and collect his entire power to follow a correct path in life, with an objective not only to reach one's goal, but to 'safely reach' at the goal on time. Unfortunately, one keeps himself careful just for a very short span of time only, and then he generally fails to keep his zeal active for long as a lesson in life.

Beware! It is the time for a person to become very careful, else he could remain at the same junction and finally he may say that, "Let my attitude be the same, I'll take care of future." But by doing so, he unknowingly and actually lags himself behind of his goals, dreams or responsibilities.

A person should observe oneself to become the follower of:

- Nature
- Bravery
- Truthfulness
- Self-respect
- Peace and Satisfaction
- Above all, the Laws of Universe

By doing so, he might get a chance to become a *Sevak* (Servant) of the community

Stage / Junction No.3
Sevak
(The servant)

S ay it to yourself . . . .
. . . . Now I want to serve for others.
and do not wait for some body to say yes . . . we need you.

In spiritual pursuits, a *Sevak* (servant) is a volunteer who comes forward to serve the humanity without any expectation in any manner what so ever.

"The charity begins at home" is an old proverb which says that, if a person wants to collect charity from others then he should contribute himself first, and later on he should ask others to donate for the charity. Similarly a person has to start from stage one of the *Sevak*.

To become a *Sevak*, when a person wish to proceed further towards the almighty, omnipresent and supernatural power called God, then one has to become a volunteer of humanity. It is the one who believes in an ideology that, "Whatever I am going to pour in as a volunteer of humanity, I will do so as I am 'capable of doing it'. I will do it without any expectation to get its result (fruit). I am genuinely going to serve and help the people who have got even the slight inclination towards truthfulness, and those who believe in God but really do not know how to proceed and in what pace and direction?"

Sevak or volunteer should help others in such a way that others should not feel obliged by him. The way of helping others should be so natural and spontaneous that it should act as one's regular basic feature of personality, and should reflect one's true compassionate feeling towards humanity. Then only, he can further find the path of Peace and Moksha.

Sevak helps and facilitates others to grow on the path of truthfulness in their lives by sharing his own knowledge, thoughts and experiences with others, in a way he has a faith in humanity.

Further after some months or years, he might get a chance to become a *Wachak* (preacher) or the narrator within this life span.

Stage / Junction No.4
Wachak
(The preacher)

If a person gets God's blessings after living as a *Sevak*, then people would start coming to him willingly for seeking his invaluable suggestions to solve their "meaningful problems" or adverse situations in life, because he possesses the virtue of truthfulness, and holds the knowledge about God. Then people would start appreciating his efforts which he extended in past few months or years. **It may be an indication that a person is turning into *Wachak* or a preacher, when he gets such natural popularity.** But it necessarily excludes the scope of giving any sort of professional suggestion which is meant to earn livelihood by him.

Listening to a preacher is generally liked by most people depending upon the nature of topic orated by him. Preachers who discourse in mass gathering, sounds very reasonable and convincing in their approach.

Listening to a favorite preacher becomes quite a happy moment for his audience or followers, and they appreciate preachers on their face. People tell openly to others that such a preacher is a wonderful person, as he knows what he talks about, and he is really a great person. It is also a fact that "following" the guidance as delivered by preacher is often seen as an uphill task by the audience, and not a few guidelines are sincerely followed by most of them. If one can follow just a single guidance then it can make a lot of difference in the life of followers.

Initially for a short time, people try to follow their preachers, but adopting such ideal thoughts into habit becomes a big task for them and followers generally give up the same later on. And next time whenever people comes in contact with the same preacher or listen to him, they tend to say happily to fellow members that, "Yes! I already know about this wonderful ideology . . . ," and they speak this just to impress their fellow members without having adopted the same into their own lives. In fact it may be better for the followers if they adopt such ideologies for betterment of their lives, than to just boast about his awareness in front of others. By adopting such invaluable ideal thoughts, the followers would not only benefit themselves but they would also get matured enough to go beyond their insensible boasting attitude, and would make their better reputation in the society by actually sharing their own real life benefits (gained by invaluable ideologies) for helping others.

Do you know why it is very difficult to follow the teachings of a preacher?

Let's understand it in a simple way. The circumstances and our belief in ourselves are actually toughened by us only, and we consider them to be more important for us than the ideal thoughts of a Preacher. We should realize the fact that we might have a role in making our own circumstances, all the resources were ours, and our belief in ourselves also concerns with our own self image. Most of the people think that these ideal thoughts hold just a bookish nature and they may not be suitable to be applied in real life. On the contrary, it is a fact that most of the man-made problems in life just arise due to neglecting the importance of applying such ideal thoughts and preachings into life, and can be taken as a timeless panacea for the upliftment of human life. Therefore, we should always have the courage to change ourselves for the betterment and good cause in life. It can easily be done by:

✓ Just keeping a farsighted view.
✓ Just becoming a visionary.
✓ Just visualize the happiness that we would gain by adopting such ideal thoughts in life.

If we really and firmly decide to adopt such positive ideas and preachings in life, then it can be said that half the job is done. For instance, by just observing clouds and feeling its cool breeze during monsoon, we get alert (in anticipation of rain) to pick up an umbrella before going out. There are indications of every coming, and it is up to us to search within the basket of our mind, as in previous topics of this book. We can obviously feel happy and relieved by taking all the preventive measures and following a positive approach in life, and by doing so we reduce or avoid adversities in life.

If we just keep all unimportant issues and negative mindset aside, and try to focus upon the matters positively that we have to do, then we can easily face almost all the situations as simple as breathing. Our life can easily become as simple as an effortless breathing.

We can observe that opportunities motivates us and time itself guides us to make a move and one should be prepared to do accordingly—physically, mentally and spiritually. Even if we consider ourselves to be self-motivated, then such a positive act must be referred as been determined by the grace of God because God is referred as a purest form and infinite source of positive energy. God is timeless as he made the time himself, and time itself is an act of God, in the same way as destiny is determined by God. So time and destiny both are the acts of God. We cannot pull our destiny to us as it naturally comes to us in its own way. We can just do an act of adopting and maintaining discipline in our lives which can truly be owed to our own credit.

One should understand the importance of discipline in life. The discipline may be taken as a way of life. Discipline not only concerns with academics and professional life, but it can be easily observed that any sort of activity, organization, institution, business or profession cannot work and prosper without discipline. The importance of observing discipline in life is so great that it becomes very difficult to achieve anything without observing the same. Discipline can be simply understood with the few examples as follows:

❖ A person simply cannot even remain healthy for long if he doesn't follow the discipline of health rules.

❖ A person cannot get rid of his illness if he doesn't follow the discipline of taking treatment and precautions as per medical advice and regimen.

❖ A person cannot even cook the food to his taste or choice if he doesn't follow the discipline of cooking the same with a well defined recipe.

❖ No matter how congested or slow the traffic moves, we avoid disobeying the discipline of traffic rules because disobeying the rules can worsen the traffic situation further.

❖ The formation of any melodious musical composition, or any sort of art, craft, drama, poetry, discourse or creative work, etc. cannot be served as an audio or visual delight without having the discipline of their respective elements, ingredients into balance, harmony and well-defined structure.

Similarly, why don't we observe and follow discipline of adopting good rules in our lives. The discipline can be applied or adopted in life in any form such as:

✓ Discipline to lead a virtuous life.
✓ Discipline not to harm or cheat others.
✓ Discipline to follow and promote law and order.
✓ Discipline to live a systematic and meaningful life.
✓ Discipline to avoid and rectify an attitude of negligence and carelessness in life.
✓ Discipline to promote and prosper healthy human relationships.
✓ Discipline to attain and maintain health, positive attitude, success and peace.
✓ Discipline to observe and practice hard work, truthfulness, dedication and patience.

In fact, discipline is such a concept which can be applied to almost any aspect of life, and it is meant to promote prosperity, balance and harmony in life.

Living life with lots of happiness may be very simple if we just follow the common sense, which is surprisingly not so common! But it is often seen that by copying or competing with others, or doing the rat race, we tend to make our life very difficult, and we do not realize of getting ourselves trapped in the vicious circle of desire and agony.

Our natural behavior and commonsense are the two great assets which we possess to live a happy, satisfied and long life.

The vicious circle of desire and agony does not allow us to make a difference between right and wrong. If we somehow realize what is wrong, then sometimes we fail to come out it even if we wish to do so, because our inner power gets consumed till then due to such negativities. We then feel powerless and have no option left other than to "wait and watch" in life.

At this junction, a person tells to himself, "My luck is very hard." One can get a solace during such time by observing an old proverb which says, "Why to cry now when the time has passed." Then the question remains, "Is there a new 'way out' to such a situation?" And its answer might be, "Yes, it may be just to restart from the scratch and put all the available power into it, then to wait for the best to come." It is possible that one might not enjoy the fruits this time, but the coming generation would get a secured future then, and they would always sing a song in praise for the same.

Beyond the stage of *Sevak*, one should reaffirm his faith in God to become a preacher. He should devote himself in exploring God and his creation. He should love all, spread happiness and stay in peace. Preacher is one who follows these things as a way of life, and further motivates others to do so.

Preacher naturally possesses some of the basic qualities such as:

- He does not take advantage of the weakness of others, but help others to overcome their weakness.
- He does not have a jealous attitude.
- He keeps his attitude cool in all conditions, especially the adverse situations.
- He keeps sharing his knowledge and experience with others for their welfare.
- He does not deliver his preachings in a style of direction or command giving manner, but in a more acceptable way of delivering the preaching in suggestive, positive and universal manner.

Capability and eagerness are the two positive factors in a person which helps him to change any circumstance. It is wiser to take the change as a development because it is an improvement in itself. One cannot satisfy himself by blaming and cursing others, and one must come out of such an attitude of satisfying himself.

If we perform an act to achieve the whole sky as our aim in the mind, and fail to get the same, then we should not get disheartened, as we surely get the moon due to such an act.

When we accomplish the job due to our capability, then we should feel happy about it. If we enjoy the task while doing it, then it gives us happiness even after the work is accomplished. It further keeps on increasing our capabilities, no matter what we get as an outcome of our efforts.

What is the objective of our life?

It may one of the most interesting questions we could ever answer in life. It is the one of the most thinkable issues indeed. An appropriate answer to this question could be, "The objective of my life is to utilize my strengths in its purest form for enhancing my knowledge about the mankind, while keeping in mind that it should not harm anybody directly or indirectly during its course."

Selfishness is not bad as long as it does not harm others in any way. One has to keep walking with above objective. The caravan may keep on increasing further by the grace of God, which may keep enhancing one's image and it must keep on moving till the last moment of life, and one should not have any regrets for anything in life.

Human life directly owes its presence to the existence of its body, having the soul as its essence or power which makes it a living being. Next comes in sequence the importance of human mind which drives him to do its Karma (action). It is the course of performing actions led by mind that lays his path to get the output (fruit). It is the virtue or quality of intentions in mind linked to one's action which leads him to his destiny.

Our mind is our best friend and the worst enemy. It is up to us that how we can keep it as our productive friend. Several times our mind and heart takes different decisions in the same situation. One should not neglect his heart (here, heart is regarded as the centre of one's feelings and emotions) because it concerns with the subconscious mind and the feelings of happiness, choices, interests, preferences, satisfaction and peace of mind associated with human life. Sometimes heart may also get the manifestation of supernatural connotations through subliminal indications of extrasensory perceptions, such as, gut feeling, intuition, premonition, etc. On the other hand, it is generally seen that the intellectuals mostly support their mind to take decisions that is not so fair.

In broad sense, it may not be appropriate for a person to hold a lifelong opinion in favor of just a particular mindset towards the heart or the mind.

Sometimes it may be a matter of common sense for us whether to make use of mind or the heart, or the balance of both, while taking decisions about different situations in life. And it is not so difficult!

> ➢ In most of the decisive situations in life, we should emphasize over the feelings of heart for gaining peace and fulfilment by doing the things of our choice and interest. It may be good to take decisions based on logic and reasoning, but it can be easily observed that all the intellectual decisions do not guarantee 100% success. Even an intellectual cannot say firmly that, "Yes, this is going to be the result." If intellectual decisions cannot guarantee success, then why should we hold such a strong inclination towards the decisions of our mind as against the feelings of heart? It doesn't mean that we should stop using the mind, the same basket which we have been filling with knowledge, wisdom and experience for years, but it is meant that we should give an importance to our gut feeling at the first place because it is the first natural option chosen by heart, and it has higher chances of gaining success than that of mind. *(It is obvious that gut feeling is instinctive in nature, and it does not include any biased opinion to make a decision.)* After taking the decision based on gut feeling, we can further intellectually utilize our mind to think, plan and follow a positive course of action for making it a success. If we really do the same in such a way, then we are more expected to see amazing and better results! In case, if the heart does not give any natural suggestion to us initially, then we can start using our mind to draw a line of plan and action, and then again wait for our heart to give us a green signal to proceed.

146

In this course, we can observe that there is an inner power which helps in making us feel comfortable, relaxed and confident. On the other hand, if we do not feel comfortable with our task, then we are less likely to become successful naturally.

> In some other decisive situations, we may try to use our mind and the hearty feelings in balance, depending upon the nature of situation. For instance, suppose if we feel inclined to have a trust or faith in somebody due to certain reasons, then it doesn't mean that we should believe him blindly. There is a big difference between a faith and blind faith. To have a belief in somebody may be a hearty, generous or noble act, but to blindly believe him may not be a wise act. We can be careful by implementing few sensible safeguards to avoid any unwelcoming situations in our lives. To become a careful person in such a case does not mean to bear unnecessary distrust, doubts or confusions in mind against the person, but it is to decently protect our own rights and interests while putting our faith over the person.

Anyone could use the common sense to deal with various such decision situations (as above) in life. Interestingly, the common sense is really a very simple thing! A person can find or follow just easy and common ways to proceed with the common sense in life. The positive and optimistic attitude, broad and open mindedness, and good observation capacity of a person can help himself to have a better common sense in life. A person with a good commonsense generally happens to be a satisfied person, due to his tendency to proceed in an easy manner.

On the other hand, many people sometimes consider it to be an inferior or substandard act to think in an easy or simple manner. Such people think that, "Thinking in an easy or common way is the fool's job because anybody could think in such manner. So what would be the extraordinary thing, if I also start thinking in an easy way?" Such thought bearing people believe that the road to success is probably very complicated and tough. I (the author) personally do not think so! We can simply observe that the laws of nature and the universe are very easy and common and nobody could make them better, other than God. Due to lack of knowledge, we make the life messy and difficult. In fact, the life is as simple as a musical note to sing.

So one should think big, think easy, use the commonsense to lead a happy life, and leave the rest to God!

147

Stage / Junction No.5
Guru
(The teacher)

(It's the Holistic approach which makes you a GURU)

To be honest, I (author) have an abundance of shortcomings which are deep-rooted inside my mind, and it is the same mind which has given me several strengths. My strengths are known to me because I utilize them timely and knowingly. My shortcomings remain with me because I act on them unknowingly. As I cannot recognize my shortcomings and therefore I cannot rectify the same. There is a hairline difference in shortcomings and strengths. My cleverness, intellect or strong vocabulary manipulates the situation to find the excuses (if I unknowingly go wrong due to my shortcomings) further convinces and satisfies me about whatever I did was right. My cleverness and command over the language overpowers me frequently.

If I wish to become a Guru, then my 1ˢᵗ Step should be to follow the process of my own self-purification and rectification, and for this purpose

I would have to recognize and support the complete truth about my own personality and character, especially regarding my shortcomings, wrongdoings and excuses (for rectifying the same).

It is our virtue and positive attitude to remain in tune with the conscience for observing, accepting and rectifying our own shortcomings and mistakes. To be able to do the same is better considered as our own strength (as against our normal strengths) in the spiritual pursuits, because it helps us in the process of self-purification.

I have come across several people. Whenever I ask people about their strengths, then they tell me about their various strengths. But when I ask them about their shortcomings, then they generally say "None" or "I do not know!" I further tell them, "Look, this is one of the shortcomings you have that you 'do not know' about yourself fully. If you observe your own inner self, then you will come to know about your shortcomings."

The basic difference in darkness and knowledge is that, darkness is big-n-huge, whereas knowledge is micro-n-minute. Recognizing the micro-n-minute is also a form of acquiring knowledge.

If a person is given unwanted or undesired knowledge, then it would be of no use to him because he tends to forget the same, whereas the knowledge of one's interest and desire is a sort of treasure, as it can be utilized by him to get its output in some way or the other.

Bad habits and shortcomings seem to be very attractive, tempting or beneficial at the initial stage, but actually they are proven to cause a very adverse or harmful effect later on.

The process of acquiring predefined knowledge and discipline seems to be very dull or tough at the initial stage, but it turns out to be very beneficial, soothing and satisfying at its effective stage.

Discoveries hold much more importance than inventions, due to the fact that inventions keep changing their formations, but discoveries works like foundations which finds out the natural or pre-existing phenomenon which remains forever. We must have the quest to discover the knowledge and the answers related to various important matters in life, such as, the *Gyan,* the Braham, ourselves and our capabilities which acts as a 2nd

Step (after the 1st Step of self-purification and rectification) towards the junction called Guru.

When we feel ourselves to be turning into Guru, or on the track of developing our personality like Guru, then first of all we may mistakenly feel ourselves to be lonely if we are on the right track. We may even feel lonely or secluded in the crowd, whether it concerns with the people of our family, friends, relatives or the profession. We may wrongly feel that nobody is with us, and rather we are there with everybody. We may feel dazed and think that negative powers are mushrooming around us. If it all happens to us, then we must take it is an opportunity given to us by the time for doing self-analysis, which is going to be our biggest power on the way to self-enhancement.

At such a stage, we should not consider our past to be better than our present. It is a suitable way to collect and motivate ourselves for start loving and accepting our present status (on our way to become a Guru). By doing so, we can use our zeal, motivation and vision to go ahead in life. It is the time for us to do self-analysis and to accept that, all people are there with us but in a different way, and we are there for everyone. People want to follow us, and they want us to share our experience with them.

It may not be important or valuable for others that what we give them as per our own choice. But, it becomes much more important for them if we give them as per their own choice or preference. Therefore, it is more appropriate to give to others as per their choice or expectations, then to think that, "I have given my best and that is what I could do, and it is up to them now whether they take it or leave it."

It is more relevant and productive that how suitable and appropriate was given to the right person at the right time.

If we do not analyze the above statements then we may turn as a proud Guru. Remember, to be proud is one of the biggest shortcomings of a human being! Now since we know about these facts, then we should get rid of such narrow mindset as quickly as possible, if we bear any such mindset. It might be difficult for anybody, but it is definitely not impossible!

A person should feel happy while analyzing oneself. He should not be grim while doing so. Happily analyzed state of mind gives satisfaction to the person, but grimly analyzed state of mind further becomes the shortcoming in itself, and may grip the person in its vicious circle.

Whether we believe it or not! When we get the answers to all such questions raised by our mind, then we put our next step towards becoming a humble Guru. (We can refer this stage to the status of Lord Gautam Buddha.)

Guru possesses a vast knowledge about various important domains, such as under:

- ✓ Astrology and its related stars, planets, sun signs, their positions, powers, and their forthcoming effects on creatures.
- ✓ Ashtanga Yoga (the 'eight-limbed' system of Yoga, as codified by the sage Patanjali) with acute clarity.
- ✓ Wide knowledge about all the four Vedas (ancient Hindu scriptures containing sacred knowledge) namely—'Rig Veda', 'Sama Veda', 'Yajur Veda' and 'Atharva Veda'.

But still he does not have the complete knowledge, because knowledge is infinite and it cannot be acquired completely.

Before we discuss about the entire potential of Guru, let's make a better platform to understand the same.

About 'Mind Power'

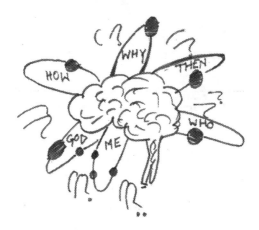

Mind is the most powerful organ we have in human body. It has two main parts—conscious mind, and subconscious mind. When we consciously train ourselves rigorously to a great extent for gaining excellence or perfection in any activity, then such an prolonged act ultimately goes into our subconscious (unconscious) mind which also gets trained during the process. Then the stage comes in our life when we can perform such activities unconsciously with full competence. It means that by reaching the unconscious level only we can become fully competent.

So the question arises, "What is the subconscious mind?"

It can be answered as, "The subconscious mind is a part of the mind of which one is not fully aware of but which influences one's actions and feelings. It also controls or is concerned with our habits. The subconscious mind is that second part of mind which is 9 times bigger than the conscious mind. In other words, it is 900% bigger than the conscious mind. It can be compared with the example of an iceberg. An iceberg is a large floating mass of ice detached from a glacier or ice sheet and carried to sea (which can be seen in Antarctica). Its 10% part is above the sea and

90% part remains submerged in the sea. Therefore the submerged part of an iceberg can be compared to the subconscious mind, whereas the tip of iceberg can be compared to the conscious mind in ratio and proportion.

When we grow consciously then our subconscious mind grows in a particular ratio and proportion. And amazingly, we can never understand the extent (size) of the effectiveness, magnitude and potential of human mind.

Guru is the one who can not only understand his mind capacity, and he can also utilize his subconscious mind as per the needs. Hence, he can step forward as a *Sant* (Saint).

To further understand the route to become a Guru. Let's reconsider all the previous topics with a new point of view. It may help those who could not understand the sequence of thoughts, and could not determine their position in life.

Another way to get Moksha as a Guru is through practicing Ashtanga Yoga.

About 'Yoga'

Yoga: It is not an unfamiliar word to us. The Yoga word comes from the Sanskrit word '*Yuj*', meaning to unite. Yoga is the union and integration of all human aspects from the subtle and innermost force to external influences that create, grow, nurture and end them. It has both practical and philosophical dimensions. The union inferred by Yoga refers not only cause intra-harmonization of body, mind and spirit, but it also causes inter-harmonization between human beings and their surroundings. Mind is quietened and purified by practicing Yoga, as it diminishes the ego in human beings which further causes the emergence of acceptance, positive feelings, joy, pure love and respect to every human being and events in life.

Man is the most responsive being amongst the whole creation. God created man with immense latent potential so that he can develop, conserve and utilize nature's gifts in favor of all the creatures. This is the fundamental thought behind the God's act. God might have **one million-trillion** reasons to create humans and other powers, but according to me (author) every reason is sufficient for each one of us to achieve Moksha. In this course, we would have new discoveries which would further improve our status to increase human level and decrease the distance from God. Any of the improvements which we bring into life (in course of Moksha) just works on the condition that they are made without harming any creature directly or indirectly.

So the question arises, "Who am I?"

As answered earlier, "I am one amongst the trillions of infinitesimally minute parts of God, into which I will merge once again. My soul was disassociated from God at his wish, to become a living being which had to pass through and develop along the course of journey (through various life cycles) in a happy, positive and optimistic way, with an ultimate aim to finally get merged into God again." Sometimes this theory does not satisfy few people. They may ask several questions about *Jeev Atma* (the

Soul). How does the Soul move? What is its source of inspiration? Where does it reside?

From time immemorial, the quest and search had always remained in the minds of human beings to answer such questions. Then came upon the stage of World "Rishi Kumar Nackhiketa", who uncovered the mystery with the help of *Yamraj* (the death executor of God), and brought forth the divine knowledge about *"Param Atma Brahma"* as the solution to such queries of mankind.

Man was happy with this solution for some time, but he further became curious again and started asking new questions, such as, "How can we get connected to *Param Atma* (God) and perceive the shape of the shapeless almighty?" As soon as this inquisitive idea emerged, intellectuals and spiritualists began the search for its solution. Various 'Rishis and Yogis' came together and acted as a team of thinkers, in such an endeavor these thinkers were the seers (*Bhavisha-drista*) who were well versed in natural sciences.

They had shown that, Yoga is the best and systematically proven science which could bridge the gap between *Jeev Atma* and *Param Atma*.

I further share my views and knowledge about 'Ashtanga Yoga' as it is known to me. I am practicing it into my life to some extent as a normal human being.

It is suggested that if anybody practices and implements it into the life, then he may easily experience its benefits as a positive and tangible difference in one's life and lifestyle.

The Guru excels in the wonderful discipline of 'Ashtanga Yoga', eight staged (limbed) Yoga. He either practices it with excellence, or has proficiency to narrate it further. His abilities then uplift himself to become a *Sant* (saint).

An overview—'Ashtanga Yoga'

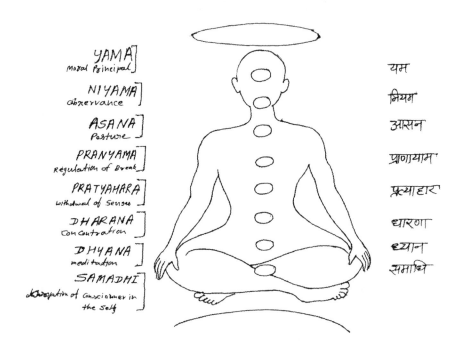

YAMA
Moral Principal

NIYAMA
observance

ASANA
Posture

PRANYAMA
Regulation of Break

PRATYAHARA
withdrawal of Senses

DHARANA
Concentration

DHYANA
meditation

SAMADHI
absorption of Consciousness in the Self

यम

नियम

आसन

प्राणायाम

प्रत्याहार

धारणा

ध्यान

समाधि

This section of book is derived from the age-old text as defined by Maharshi Patanjali, re-narrated and re-explained here.

Human life has the following four *Avastha*s (parts):

1. *Bal Avastha*   Age 0-21 yrs.:   (Childhood)
2. *Grahasth Avastha*   Age 22-60 yrs.:   (Family life)
3. *Vanprasth Avastha*   Age 61-74 yrs.:   (Giving up social life)
4. *Sanyas Avastha*   Age 74-Till end of life: (Total spirituality)

Ashtanga Yoga begins at *Avastha* stage 1 and continues up to *Avastha* stage 4.

Ashtanga Yoga means Yoga of 8 limbs (stages) as follows:

1. *Yama* (Moral codes or principles)
2. *Niyama* (Personal disciplines)
3. Asana (postures—this is what at large taken as YOGA)
4. Pranayama (Regulation of Breath)
5. *Pratyahara (withdrawal of senses)*
6. *Dharana (Concentratión)*
7. *Dhyana (Meditation)*
8. Samadhi (Knowingly reliving Consciousness of physical and mental body)

These 8 limbs (stages) can be spelt as 'YNAP-PDDS' in short as an acronym, to memorize easily.

Every limb (stage) of Ashtanga Yoga has a full description to live. It is actually "The Great Journey" very systematically defined, and all of its 8 limbs (stages) are the junctions as stated before. For a common man like you and me, let's discuss these stages briefly one by one.

If we make an inspiring environment of Ashtanga Yoga in our families for the kids to follow such a great heritage, as it used to happen in India centuries ago during the era of Rishis, then we can help our next generations to reach at its far greater stages than what we could not attain in our lives, in the present scenario of life. In case we begin to follow the rules of Ashtanga Yoga now, then we really have to restart our lives from zero level. If God blesses a person to live few additional years than what is written in his destiny, then he could reach up to 8th limb (stage) of Ashtanga Yoga. Reaching such a great stage is actually very difficult, but it is possible!

Its fundaments are well defined in the *Kathopanishad, Bhagawad Gita* and *Yoga Sutras.* These fundamental principles of Yoga—both in theory and practice are known as 'Classical Yoga' or 'Ashtanga Yoga'.

The 8 limbs (stages) of Ashtanga Yoga can be classified into three Heads:

First Head classification: It covers two limbs (1st and 2nd limb) of Ashtanga Yoga which are about Yogic ethics, as follows:

1. *Yama* (moral codes or principles): It is 1st limb (stage) of Ashtanga Yoga. It further describes five moral sub-codes.
2. *Niyama* (personal disciplines): It is 2nd limb (stage) of Ashtanga Yoga. It further describes five personal sub-disciplines.

Second head classification: It covers three limbs (3rd, 4th and 5th limb) of Ashtanga Yoga, which are about external Yogic practices:

3. Asana (art of postures)
4. Pranayama (science of breath)
5. *Pratyahara*

Third head: It covers three limbs (6th, 7th and 8th limb) of Ashtanga Yoga, which are about Internal or Meditative practices:

6. *Dharana* (concentration)
7. *Dhyana* (Meditation)
8. Samadhi

The 8 limbs are explained as follows:

1. **Yama (moral codes or principles):** It is 1st limb (stage) of Ashtanga Yoga. *Yama* further describes five moral codes or principles which should be followed in life. These five moral codes can be spelt as 'ASABA' in short as an acronym to memorize easily, under which we learn:

   1.1 Ahimsa (non-violence)
   1.2 *Satya* (truth)
   1.3 *Asteya* (non-stealing)
   1.4 *Brahmacharya* (sexual continence)
   1.5 *Aparigraha* (non-possessiveness)

   1.1 Ahimsa (non-violence): With the help of principle of ahimsa, Mahatma Gandhi brought freedom to our nation India. It is the universal moral commandment, and it is considered as an ethical preparation for a student of Yoga. The basic principle of ahimsa is not to harm any living being by any means. It promotes the feeling of universal love and brotherhood which makes one's mind pure. To reprobate the feeling of hatred from anyone is also a part of non-violence.

1.2 *Satya* (truth): The principle of *satya* (truth) holds the universal importance. It is the only uncontroversial basis for the development of self. Mahatma Gandhi once said, "Truth is God, and God is truth." The importance of *satya* can be compared to the fire with an example that, "Fire burns the impurities in a process of refining gold, and then the refined gold is obtained." Similarly, fire of truth cleans our inner self. If one thinks about truth and speaks the truth, then he naturally moves one step ahead towards union with the almighty God. Truth and love holds an ultimate importance in this world, and Yoga disciplines them in not only the speech and theory but also in a routine conduct and practical way. Untruthfulness drifts a person from his mission to success & Bliss.

1.3 *Asteya* (non-stealing): *Asteya* is the principle which puts emphasis on an act to desist the desire of stealing or using other's belongings, whether money, material or ideas for one's own benefit. Such a concept of non-stealing includes, not taking or using the belongings of others without their prior permission, and also not using the borrowed item for other purpose or using it beyond the time period as permitted by its lender. It further desist the misuse, misappropriation, mismanagement of any belongings of others, or the misconduct, breach of trust among people. *Asteya* not only gives mental peace and self-purification to an individual, but it also reduces several social tensions and evils. One should reduce one's needs to a minimum to achieve the ability to ward off great temptations. An old proverb in Hindi says, *"Apni roti kha kar thanda pani pi, dekh parai chupdi mat lalcho jeev."* It means, "Let's be satisfied with what you have earned, rather feeling jealous by what others have achieved."

1.4 *Brahmacharya* (sexual continence): The basic principle of abstain components of *brahmacharya* is to live the life of a celibate by remaining pure and virtuously self-restrained in sexual deeds and thoughts, and to perform religious acts. It does not mean to remain celibate by preserving semen, or to strictly abstain from sexual activity or the marriage. Instead, to practice celibacy in terms of becoming pure in one's thoughts and actions, and **not to lead a** sexually perverted, indecent, immoral, illicit, lustful or sinful life. Today, we can witness the "ill effects" of sexually degraded, unrestraint, immoral, illicit behaviour and activities of human beings, which results in the occurrence of sexual offences, and it has also caused millions of people to suffer various sexually transmitted diseases, including the incurable AIDS. In the process of attaining purity of mind, moral edification and sexual continence, a *brahmachari* (one who practices *brahmacharya*) can easily transform, alter or redirect his course of thinking and natural flow of sexual energy towards one's own spiritual upliftment, or elevating the other aspects of life. The concept of *brahmacharya* is not a negation, forced austerity or prohibition to the sexual life.

Maharshi Patanjali stated that, "The real *brahmacharya* lays stress on the continence of body, speed and mind." It has little to do with a person's marital status or living a common man's life. It is open for one and all, irrespective of age, cast, creed, class and gender. It is not at all necessary for a human being to suppress his natural sexual instincts or stay unmarried in order to attain salvation, because one can enter into marital relation for enjoying companionship, solely for the creation of progeny or for having a virtuously self-restrain sexual life, and thus still remain a *brahmachari*. Therefore the *brahmacharya* includes the scope of leading a virtuously self-restrained marital life. Multiple amorous relations are performed by animals, whereas human being surely is a far better *Jeev*.

1.5 *Aparigraha* (**non-possessiveness**): To remain free from the mindset or an act of hoarding anything is called *aparigraha*. A Yogic disciple should keep his desires as minimum as possible. Some of the materialistic possessions may be good to support the needs and necessities of life, but anything accumulated in excess or a desire of acquiring unwanted new versions of anything is regarded as the poison to mankind, as per the philosophy of Yoga. A true Yogic disciple does not need a lot of things at a particular point of time. Hence he should not hoard or collect things. The unnecessary or excess collection of things for future need shows the lack of faith in God and in oneself because the Almighty God who looks after the whole creations will fulfil and meet our requirements timely. One can make his life happy simply by following the norms of *aparigraha* where there is no fear or lack of trust.

Life of a common man is full of miseries, disturbances, agonies and frustrations, which keeps his mind always in a state of imbalance and perturbation. Basic reasons for such a condition are his failure to fulfil extreme desires or the fear to lose something which he has hoarded for luxuries or the future. Such an act does not mean that one should stop working for upgrading his living standard, but it means to develop oneself while keeping any extreme or "unrealistic desire" in control. Observance of *aparigraha* enables a person to be satisfied with whatever he has and whatever happens to him. He achieves peace which takes him beyond the realms of illusion and misery. His mind is always calm, cool, unperturbed and in a state of equilibrium.

Once, a Guru and his few disciples were sitting together. Guru asked to all of them, "Do you know about how long each one of you would live? Please tell me about it."

One of his disciple replied, "May be till the age of 85 years."

Another replied, "I can't say whether I would see even tomorrow or not."

A third disciple replied, "May be till this evening."

When Guru asked the same question to the forth one, he replied, "Sir, you only tell us I have no clues . . ."

Guru then replied, "Your death may be just 6 inches away from you, from your nose to your lungs. One cannot be sure whether the next breath he would be able to breathe or not."

Philosophy of *aparigraha* refers to the truth about such uncertainty of human life. A person should perform his duties and actions to the fullest while keeping one's desires in control so that even if he dies on the next moment of life, then he would die "satisfied and successful". Success is not a destination where one reaches but it is a state of "satisfied mind" that one carries.

2. ***Niyama* (Personal disciplines):** It is 2nd limb (stage) of Ashtanga Yoga. *Niyama* further describes five personal disciplines which should be followed in life. These five personal disciplines can be spelt as 'SSTSI' in short as an acronym to memorize easily, under which we learn:

2.1 *Shaucha* (purity)
2.2 *Santosh* (contentment)
2.3 *Tapa* (penance)
2.4 *Swadhyaya* (Self-study)
2.5 *Ishwar pranidhan* (God realization)

2.1 *Shaucha* (purity): The purity of physical body is essential for our well-being. At the same time, cleansing the mind of its disturbing emotions like hatred, passion, anger, lust, greed, delusion and pride are equally important. Cleansing the intellect of impure and unhealthy thoughts is equally important. The toxins and impurities of body are removed by pranayama and asanas. They not only clean the body but also tone the entire body along with doing its rejuvenation. The impurities of mind may be washed off by adopting devotion (bhakti), whereas the imprints of intellect are removed or burned off in the fire of self-study *(swadhyaya)*. Purification or cleansing of physical body, mind and intellect brings the state of benevolence *(saumanasya)* which banishes mental pain, dejection, sorrow, despair, and gives the satisfaction with joy. In this condition, a person is able to concentrate one's mind to have victory over one's own senses. Thereafter, he enters the sacred temple of his own body and sees his real self in the mirror of his mind.

Food is the basic necessity of body. The right kind of balanced and nutritious food is necessary to keep the body and mind healthy. One should be very careful about how his food is procured, how it is prepared and in what way it is consumed? For a Yoga disciple, a vegetarian diet is essential in order to attain concentration and spiritual evolution. Food is eaten to promote health, to get energy, strength, and for the purpose of self rejuvenation only. Hence, the food should be simple, nourishing, juicy, soothing and with all necessary nutrients like, carbohydrates, proteins, vitamins, minerals and roughages. One should remember that, his each meal should have a balance of sour, bitter, salty, pungent and sweet taste in it, which makes it a complete food. But excess of anything should be avoided. Besides food, our habitat is equally important for spiritual practise and healing purposes. It should be free from insects and noise pollution, should be clean, airy, dry, and with sufficient sunlight.

2.2 *Santosh* (contentment): The feeling of contentment must be there in one's mind. A person cannot concentrate when he becomes greedy. The concept of *Santosh* (contentment) does not discourage a person to think about his materialistic desires, growth and development, but it redirects a person to think about attaining the wealth and success in a virtuous way (i.e., without any greed or unfair means) while keeping a balanced state of mind and feeling happy in whatever the condition he lives, and enjoy whatever the wealth he possesses on the path to progress further. One should be contented with whatever he owns or gets, and should be grateful to God for his grace. Cast, creed and wealth are generally the major factors for dissatisfaction among people, and these factors lead to conscious or subconscious conflicts. In such conditions, mind cannot concentrate or think single-minded *(ekagra)*. As a result, mind is deprived of its peace which is not the way of tranquility, truth and joy, and in their absence any kind of virtuous success cannot be achieved.

Here we discuss about the way to bliss.

2.3 *Tapa* (penance): The effort and practice of building the character may be termed as *tapa*. It means to burn, shine, consume, blaze or destroy all kinds of pains with the help of inner self and control of energy. It is a process of burning the desires that stands in the way of achieving the ultimate goal of life. *Tapa* involves self-purification, self-discipline and austerity, and is a conscious effort to achieve the ultimate union with the divine power. There are three types of *tapa* (penances), which may be related to body *(kayika)*, speech *(vachika)* or mind *(mansika)*.

- Penances of body: *Brahmacharya* (continence) and *ahimsa* (non-violence).

163

- Penances of speech: Always speaking truth without thinking of its consequences, using the words that do not offend others, and reciting the glory of almighty God.
- Penances of mind: To keep tranquil and balanced in both joy and sorrow, and always have self-control.

The fundamental principle of *tapa* is to work without any selfish motive or to work without any hope to get a reward. *Tapa* helps in developing a strong body, mind and character, which yields courage, wisdom, straightforward simplicity and integrity.

2.4 *Swadhyaya* (self-study): The process of educating oneself is *swadhyaya*. Education is a process that gives us knowledge and information in its respective field, and helps us to bring out or optimally develop the hidden potentials of our various mental faculties, including, the intellect, rationality, creativity, personality, talents, maturity and confidence. It also helps us to live a well-mannered, cultured and sensible life. It may further help to enhance the Intelligence Quotient (IQ), Emotional Quotient (EQ), Spiritual Quotient (SQ), etc in some way or the other to some extent, with respect to the acquired or applied knowledge, practice and acumen.

In a process of *swadhyaya*, the concerned person is both the speaker as well as the listener. It is not similar to a classroom lecture where the lecturer speaks before the audience of students who follow the instructions. In *swadhyaya*, a person speaks and listens to himself. His mind and heart are full of love and respect. The noble thoughts arising from this practice gets assimilated to become a part of one's being. You might have heard about Gautam Buddha. *Swadhyaya* changes the outlook of life. A person starts believing that life is not meant for the enjoyment only, but life is an opportunity to find out the meaning and purpose of one's own existence, all the creations are divine and life is meant for adoration. He starts thinking that, there is a part of divinity within himself, and this source of energy which is engraved in him is given by God, while the same energy is flowing in others too.

Acharya Vinoba Bhave once said, "*Swadhyaya* is the study of one's own selves which is the root of all other subjects upon which the others rest, but which itself does not rest upon anything else."

To lead a happy, healthy, peaceful and spiritual life, it is necessary to develop the habit of reading the edifying and divine literature. It brings the misconceptions and ignorance to an end. This habit enables a person to understand the nature of his soul and to establish the link with divine.

2.5 *lshwar pranidhan* **(God realization):** *Ishwara pranidhana* is an act of dedicating all of the one's actions, efforts, wishes, possessions, achievements, success, etc to the God. Anyone who believes in God knows that all the creation belongs to God. By appreciating this fact, one would not face any dilemma and would not be puffed up with the pride of power and success, and he would always bow his head only in worship of God. Our senses are gratified with greed and attachment, and any hindrance in the process leads us to sorrow, which can be curbed with the help of knowledge and forbearance in a full conscious state only. The conscious state is directly governed by mind, and it is very difficult to control mind which needs extra resources that can be obtained from God. And for that, one has to take the shelter of God with full honesty and dedication. It is the phase where devotion (bhakti) begins. In the process of bhakti, the mind, intellect, will and wish are made humbly subservient to God with a prayer that, "I am nothing and almighty will take care of me." Bhakti concerns with the process of detaching 'I' and 'mine' from oneself, and about the presence of true love and devotion towards God. It leads the soul of an individual to have its full growth. When a mind is filled with thoughts of personal gratification, then there is always a danger that senses tends to drag the mind towards the objects of desire. But when a mind is emptied of the desires of personal gratification, then a mind can easily be filled with bhakti of God. Such a way of bhakti enables a person to proceed in the right direction of conduct and attaining knowledge, because the name of God is like a sun dispelling darkness. When the moon of our life faces the sun, it glows like a full moon.

3. Asanas (Art of postures): Asana or posture is the 3rd limb of Maharshi Patanjali's Ashtanga Yoga. Asanas are well described in

Hath Yoga Pradipika where it has been placed 1st in the sequence of Yoga practice. *Mandal Brahmopanishad* describes, "The posture in which one can sit comfortable for an indefinite period is called asana." Whereas, Patanjali describes it as *Sthir Sukhasanam* which means, "The posture in which one can sit comfortable and steadily is called asana." Asana brings real steadiness, health and easiness to all body parts, which ultimately brings mental equipoise and peace. They are altogether different from gymnastic exercises. One does not need any infrastructure facility or equipments to perform asanas, as in case of games or gymnastic exercises. It can be performed alone and anywhere without any specific preparation. What is needed is only a small blanket, a clean and airy space and self-confidence. By practicing the asanas, one can develop physical health, endurance, vitality and can achieve longevity due to perfect health.

Asanas are classified in three categories:

1.   Meditative asanas.
2.   Asanas providing mental tranquillity.
3.   Asanas providing physical strength.

Asanas falling in first category are practiced before meditation. They are most suitable postures for doing meditation session. The second category of asansa provide total mental peace and tranquilly, and prevents fickleness of mind. The third category of asanas is practiced to get physical strength and body power. Asanas have been evolved over the centuries, so as to exercise every muscle, nerve and gland in the body. They help in securing a find physique, which is strong and elastic without being muscle bound and they keep the body free from disease. They also reduce fatigue and sooth the nerves but their real importance lies in the way they train and discipline the mind.

4.   **Pranayama (science of breath):** Pranayama is the 4th limb of Ashtanga Yoga. It is the process of yogic breath or science of breath. As stated in Yoga sutra, "*tasmin sati shwas prashws yorgati vichchhedah pranayamah*," it says that pranayama is related with prana, which means the breath, respiration, life vitality, wind, energy or strength. The suffix "ayam" means length, expansion stretching or restraint. Pranayama thus means the extension of breath along with the control.

Every breath has three phases or components:

1. ***Puraka* (to fill):** It is an Inhalation or inspiration phase.
2. ***Kumbhaka:*** It is a conscious retention or holding phase, a state when the inspired air is held in the lungs.
3. ***Rechaka* (to empty):** It is an exhalation or expiration phase, in which the filled air is released smoothly from the lungs.

There are two states of *Kumbhaka* phase of breath: *Abhyantara kumbhaka* and *Bahya kumbhaka*. In *Abhyantara kumbhaka*, the *sadhak* (seeker) withholds the breath after the inhalation phase of *Puraka*, whereas in *Bahya kumbhaka* he withholds the breath after the exhalation phase of *Rechaka*.

In pranayama, there is a measured timing ratio for the three stages and the ratio should be carefully observed.

In Yogic breathing, *puraka* (inhalation phase) consists of muscular action. The movement has two parts working together. In the first part, the thoracic cage expands to make room for lungs to inflate, while in the second part, the dome shaped diaphragm descends to a flat position which swells out the abdomen and benefits the abdominal viscera by giving them a mild massage. One should pour the air deeply into the lungs while breathing, but the end point of inhalation and expansion should be just before the point at which discomfort intrudes. If one sits easily with the back straight and level head position, then his respiratory muscles are in a good position to expand and recoil properly, which enables an act of doing the pranayama comfortably.

Holding of breath is a conscious act that checks the mechanism, whereby our respiration is automatically regulated. With the *kumbhaka* (conscious suspension of breath), we just switch from 'automatic' to a 'self-controlled' breathing mode for the few moments while doing it. It requires some practice for gaining smoothness and ease in this act, the criteria of which is to refrain from force and discomfort while doing the same. When *kumbhaka* follows, filling of the lungs or thoracic umbrella must stay open, with diaphragm down and the abdomen out during the breathing pause. One has to inhibit the initial recoiling tendency of ribs and diaphragm during the moments of both the full lungs and empty lungs pauses at *abhyantara kumbhaka* and *bahya kumbhaka* respectively. However, after some weeks of training, inhibition becomes effortless as long as *kumbhaka* is not prolonged up to a point of strain. During *kumbhaka* with full lung or empty lung, one should resist the temptation to let a little air pass through the nostrils or mount to keep the suspension going comfortably. The abdomen should not change the tone of contracting or relaxing. Yogic breath suspension *(kumbhaka)* achieves both physiological and psychological benefits. The pause gives more time for the gaseous exchange of oxygen into carbon dioxide across blood capillaries. In addition, it allows better exchange of fresh air with stale residual air in the alveolar sacs of lungs. Holding of breath during the period when lungs are filled has a cleansing and purifying effect on residual air.

In Pranayama, comprehensive time is allowed to empty the lungs, as to fill them. Carbon dioxide is a waste gas that all the cells of body exchange for fresh oxygen every three minutes, and it is expelled from the body with every outgoing breath. Some residual air remains as mentioned earlier. The more complete and efficient exhalation enables better and efficient purification by greater lung expansion, inflow of fresh air and oxygen on the following inspiration.

5. **Pratyahara (sensual control):** *Pratyahara* is the 5th limb of Ashtanga Yoga. Senses are the basic source of all sensual tyrannies, and if a man has a firm and rhythmic control over his senses, then he may be free from several agonies caused by them. Practicing of *pratyahara* brings all the senses under one's own control and discipline. Bhakti of God finds a way to defeat the materialistic attractions of sensual objects in the world. In fact, man's mind is the central point around which all the pleasures or pains, liberation or bondage, happiness or sorrow keeps on revolving continuously. There may be bondage, pain or sorrow if one's mind indulges into greed or grieves over any specific subject matter, and on the other hand, one may feel pleasure, liberation and happiness if his mind becomes free from all greed, attachments and fears. Purpose of life should be to acquire the 'good' instead of 'pleasant', whereas a common man generally tries to get the pleasant, and ignores the sacred element in precious life. The ultimate aim of *pratyahara* is to achieve the good and sacred in life. A person feels joy and satisfaction by practicing *pratyahara*

because he knows how to stop and where to go, what to accept and what to reject. He understands that whatever may feel bitter like a poison today, will definitely become sweet tomorrow.

A man observing the principles of Yoga knows that the path of sensual satisfaction and desire fulfillment goes straight to destruction, whereas to tread the path of Yoga is like walking on the sharp edge of a razor. It is a narrow and difficult path to tread, and there are very few people who follow it, although it is the only path of salvation and it is possible to walk upon.

A person experiences the fullness of creation or the creator by observing *pratyahara*. His blind search for the objects of senses ends, and he looks at them with dispassion ever after then. He remains stable in any conditions of pleasure or pain, virtue or vice, honor or dishonor. He remains in a state of equanimity and experiences the fullness of universal soul, and such a condition of attitude and behavior leads him to the path of perfection.

6. *Dharana* (**concentration**): It is the 6th limb of Ashtanga Yoga. *Dharana* is to put the concentration of mind over a single point, or to put total attention on what is being done at any particular moment. The mind remains focused and unruffled by doing so. It stimulates the inner awareness to integrate the ever flowing intelligence and releases all the tensions. In fact, one cannot unlock the divinity within oneself or become a universal man without concentrating on divinity which shapes and controls the universe.

A person's mind should be a willing servant of oneself, but there are very rare people who possess natural self-discipline for achieving control over their own minds. It is usual for most of us that mind is either a helpless slave or a tyrannical master. We all may get time affected by the worldly abuses due to the lack of adequate orientation. Some of us let ourselves be buffeted by emotional storms or be distracted by external stimuli with a result that, single-minded pursuit of what is truly important to us becomes impossible to achieve. Few others tend to veer to other extreme in an effort to set up deafness against external or emotional distractions. As mentioned in the earlier pages of this "Blue Book", we become creatures of the mind exclusively and ignore our natural impulses. Thus it becomes very difficult for us to self-discipline ourselves, and the negation of which depletes our energy that could more conveniently be put to constructive, creative or better uses. Such basic failures of human nature are as old as human nature itself. Yogis were wisely aware of such failures and so they devised a method of dealing with such problems long ago, and it is the basis of practice *Dharana.*

In the process of concentration, one must concentrate on 'something'. It is obvious that there can be no such thing like a mental vacuum. One should try to focus one's attention on some image or object while determinedly shutting out everything else. In this process, mind is directed to focus closely, firmly and steadily on any particular object or image, and then one can achieve its perfection slowly and gradually by practicing the same. One must keep his mind serene to concentrate properly, which means emptying the mind of irritations, worries, distractions, and not permitting any of such negative emotions to take hold of mind which could interfere with the desired goals or the peace of mind. It is simply a matter of practice. When anybody tries to concentrate on the object of one's choice, one will find immediate preconceptions of daily life influencing the mental faculty to shut out deliberately. In this process, one should learn to watch his thought dispassionately and objectively as if he is just like an interested spectator, but he should not permit himself to get attached with such thoughts. When the thoughts begin to wander, then one should divert his thoughts into right direction. It may seem dull and uninspiring at first but the practice of day dreaming or visualizing any activity, such as, wool gathering may be more attractive pastimes to concentrate upon, or focusing at the flame of candle may also be a good option. Any such practice to gain concentration may soon yield rewards. It becomes surprising later on that, how quickly a little mechanical exercise may enable a person to discipline his mind when he is required to focus on something important and vital in life. As a result mind will no longer be tempted to wander at all.

7. ***Dhyana*** (**Meditation**)**:** It is the 7ᵗʰ limb of Ashtanga Yoga. Meditation is the practice of taking one's own mind into constant observation. It means focusing the mind at one point or stilling the mind in order to perceive oneself. By stopping or disciplining the uncontrolled and turbulent waves of thoughts, a person may realize his own true nature or discover the wisdom and tranquility

that lies within oneself. It is like a phenomenon of focusing the rays of Sun with a magnifying glass makes them hot enough to burn an object. Similarly, focusing the scattered energy of thought makes the mind penetrating and powerful. One can discover a greater purpose in life, strengthen the will power, and one's thinking becomes clearer and more concentrated with the continued practice of meditation, which affects a person and all his actions. Swami Vishnu Devananda has written, "The state of meditation does not come easily. It is something like a beautiful tree that grows and blossoms slowly, and one has to wait for its blossom and ripening of fruits to enjoy the ultimate taste of fruits. Similarly, the blossom of meditation is an expressible peace that permeates one's entire being. The ecstatic feeling of its wonderful peace and spiritual essence is indescribable." I have enjoyed and experienced the wonderful benefits of meditation before writing this book, and I am sure that if you try and continue to meditatively focus and observe the "subject" matter, then you will also enjoy its benefits in the due course of your life.

Using concentration as a tool, the next and final step towards true self-mastery is meditation. Yogic teachings describes that an individual can learn to become truly and fully conscious of oneself through meditation. He identifies oneself as a separate and distinct entity which is different from all the other manifestations of life. Such a special recognition of one's identity is not at all in the form of highly personal and individualistic Western philosophical sense (which may often misdirect a person to egocentricity and uneasy self-absorption). Whereas a person of distinct identity (as evolved through meditation) interacts with others in a detached way that actually makes oneself immune to the superficial influences. Common man is subjected to frequent competitive pressures, and gets influenced by the fears and insecurities caused by them. He easily becomes a prey to anxiety or feels panic while trying to achieve very tough social standards which are artificially set by his milieu. **On the other hand, people who wisely take time to find out about their purpose of life, quickly lose their need to play the life-long game of following the leader.** Such people learn to differentiate between "What is right and what is wrong for them", "What they really want out of life, and what they have been made to believe they want." They learn to be true to themselves, and feel liberated with such conformity due to such awareness.

It is a fact that a person who has learned to sort out the confusions after having stayed with his problems for a long period, tends to thoughtfully change his own attitude further. First of all, he must discover one's own true 'identity' out of unnecessary clutter of superimposed images. Then he must decide after doing an analysis about, which of his problems he may be able to solve, and with which problems he must learn to live within the light of objective reality. Once a person attains such knowledge about oneself, and develops the capacity of self-analysis, then he automatically feels himself to come out of situation which was something like hitting one's head against the wall. The inner sense of serenity will replace senseless turmoil.

There are two types of meditations:

1. *Saguna* (concrete) meditation.
2. *Nirguna* (abstract) meditation.

In *saguna* meditation, one tries to focus on any concrete object at which the mind easily dwells upon an image or a visual symbol.

In *nirguna* meditation, the point of focus is an abstract idea, such as, the absolute concept that is indescribable in words.

8. **Samadhi:** Samadhi is the 8th limb of Ashtanga Yoga. It is the peak of Yogi's quest. When a Yogi reaches the height of meditation, he then enters into the state of Samadhi. At this stage, his body and bodily senses are at complete rest as if one is in state of sleep, although his mental faculties are fully alert as if he has attained the state of super consciousness. In fact, Yogi loses consciousness of his body, breath, intelligence and ego when he enters into the state of Samadhi. He lives in an infinite peace where his wisdom and purity gets combined with simplicity and humility. Then such of his colossal virtue shines him in spiritual pursuits.

I could write only this much here with the knowledge of whatever I learned, practised, experienced and read from various books. The realm of Ashtanga Yoga is so comprehensive that it requires a separate book to be written in detail about such a great topic. Guru has the entire knowledge of Ashtanga Yoga. The stage of a Guru will be described in my next volume of "Blue Book" in detail. Beyond the stage of a Guru, the stages of Panthik and

Gyanendra would be the main part of my next "Blue Book: Volume 2".

If these stages are properly understood by all of us and if we apply them in our daily life, then we may find ourselves to be on the way to attain super success in life, and also the "Moksha" or the ultimate peace called "Bliss". In fact most of the people really do not know about what to do or how to attain all of these stages? Therefore all the topics and their suitable examples in this book can be viewed as a ready reference to attain the "Bliss".

The Guru is one who possesses in-depth understanding of all the stages, topics (as mentioned in this book) and all the aspects of Ashtanga Yoga in their real form itself, and he is proficient in passing it to the coming generations.

In next volume "Blue Book: Volume 2", you will find Junction No.5 in very well elaborated form, and the beginning stage of Junction No.6.

I could write a brief expression as I am discovering and developing my knowledge to elaborate Junction No. 5. Beyond this stage, there are many stages (please refer to initial pages) for which I am observing, studying several aspects of life and meditating to understand these stages, so that I can put them in words in the simplest manner.

<u>End of SECTION—4</u>

QUEST—Increase your hunger for knowledge

QUEST-MAN

If you find this book interesting, then hunger for knowledge in this respective field can further be increased. The "Blue Book: Volume 2" will soon be published to serve the readers.

We can brain-storm ourselves with the questions in search of knowledge like "Gautam Buddha" did, and can get the answers one after another.

Although in the starting pages of this book several such questions were written to enhance your curiosity, but to assist you a bit more—you can begin like this too, just ask yourself any meaningful question which was never put to you by anyone or by you to others. If such questions are formed, then try to answer them. Your answer should end on Almighty God and then only the answer would be complete, because there is no answer beyond God and this is how you may uplift your spiritual knowledge or enlighten yourself, and decrease the distance from the

God and the Moksha. Such questions could be somewhat like these as under:

Question 1: If desire is the mother of invention, then who is the mother of discovery?

Answer 1: Eagerness or curiosity is the mother of discovery.

Question 2: Who is the mother of curiosity?

Answer 2: Vision is the mother of curiosity.

Question 3: Who is the mother of vision?

Answer 3: Faith is the mother of vision.

Question 4: Who is the mother of faith?

Answer 4: Self-confidence is the mother of faith.

Question 5: Who is the mother of self-confidence?

Answer 5: Observation and basic fundamentals of life is the mother of self-confidence.

Question 6: Who is the mother of basic fundamentals of a person?

Answer 6: Education and the stars of astrology make the basic fundamentals of a person.

Question 7: Who is the mother of stars of astrology?

Answer 7: Brahma is the mother (creator) of stars of astrology.

Question 8: Who is Brahma?

Answer 8: The power of creation is Brahma, who creates on the basis of several million effects on and of the universe.

Question 9: Who creates the effects to the universe?

<u>Answer 9</u>: '*Atma* of the living body' and '*Paramatma* with the supernatural power', both effects the universe.

<u>Question 10</u>: What is the supernatural power?

<u>Answer 10</u>: *Jal, Vayu, Akash, Agni and Prithvi (panchtatva)* together are the manifestations of supernatural power.

<u>Question 11</u>: Who made these *Panchbhoot*?

<u>Answer 11</u>: The Almighty God.

<u>The other type of Questions we may ask to ourselves</u>:

<u>Question 1</u>: Who am I?

<u>Answer 1</u>: I am an offspring of my parents who gave me the physical body, and I have a soul in this body given by God. I am called a living being. Since I am from the community of humans, and so I am called a human being.

<u>Question 2</u>: What is the soul?

<u>Answer 2</u>: Soul is a very tiny (super nano) or an infinitesimal part of the supernatural power called God.

<u>Question 3</u>: Why it is called a tiny part of God?

<u>Answer 3</u>: It is the spiritual or immaterial part of a human being or animal, regarded as immortal. The soul does not have its own materialistic form, so its tiny part is not visible through any type of apparatus such as powerful microscope which can otherwise help us to see the nano parts of creatures. At the death of human or living being, the soul leave its body and it either goes back to get dissolved into God or it switches over to a new body. Hence, it is called a tiny (super nano) part of the supernatural power called Almighty God.

Both of the above 2 sessions of Questions finally ends on the importance of God. Similarly, if your question and answer session also ends on God at the end of every sequence of thought (as above), then the probability of your answers to be correct increases. Then you would

176

be closer to the Almighty God, and gradually you would get dissolved in God.

The fulfillment of one's wish to reunite with the supernatural power is called Moksha or Bliss.

Here are few more questions which are not answered, and it is suggested that you should first try to search the answers to the following questions at your own. (If you don't find their answers, then these questions can be answered by me on written request, or in my "Blue Book-II")

Question 1: Why I am not as successful as others?

Question 2: Why do we have to suffer due to illness?

Question 3: What can I do when I have no hope left?

Question 4: How can I become what I thought a few years back?

Question 5: What is the top most situation of peaceful life?

Question 6: When I would become a rich person?

Question 7: When I would attain cool and comfortable life despite having everything with me?

Question 8: Why do people often tell lies to me?

Question 9: Why are people friendly with me but not helpful when desired?

Question 10: Why my relations with masses and my relatives are not good?

Question 11: What is the aim of my life?

Question 12: How to know what is my capacity to grow?

Question 13: What will happen to this mad world? I am totally confused . . . !

<u>Question 14</u>: How long do I have to remain in this situation of my life, how can I improve it?

<u>Question 15</u>: Why do people appreciate them who are actually not so good but show off a lot?

<u>Question 16</u>: Why people are not really thankful towards me despite of my being genuine and true towards them?

*   *   *

I have tried to frame several questions as above, so as to serve them as a sample to the reader and to give an idea about framing such questions.

There could be thousands of better questions than as mentioned above. **Think it over and storm your brain!**

This book can be re-read for better understanding. The "Blue Book" ends here, but its next volume will soon be available for the readers.

I wish you all the best for a smooth, successful and happy life, and also for the way to attain Bliss!

Thank a lot for sparing out the time to read this book.

Good bye for now!

*   *   *

Feedback

I would appreciate your efforts

Please provide your feedback preferably in writing at <u>www.rohitbluebook.com</u>. In case you find it difficult to write, kindly call on any of these numbers. Your feedback may provide me an idea of understanding the reader better and I would like to rectify the language, vocabulary, flow of writing or zest of the book.

For your convenience, I am enclosing the feedback format. You may use it and oblige me.

After your due approval, I would like to put your remarks on the jacket of my next "Blue Book" as a testimony for the new readers. Your kind and generous efforts in giving the remarks or suggestions would become an added asset to this book.

Thanks,

Rohit Kumar Vohra
F-46, RIICO bais godam Industrial area, Jaipur 302006 (INDIA)
Telephone: +91-141-2219129(Office) Jaipur
Mobile: +91 98290 00096
The "Blue Book" feedback can be e-mailed at:
<u>author@mybluebook.in</u>

RE—READ THIS BOOK AS FREQUENTLY AS YOU CAN